SAVVY SAVINGS GUIDE

for home and business

Paying for College

Get An Education without Breaking the Bank!

J.K.LASSER INSTITUTE

Barbara Wagner

WILEY

John Wiley & Sons, Inc.

Published by John Wiley & Sons, Inc., Hoboken, New Jersey
Published simultaneously in Canada

For general information on our other products and services, or technical support, please contact our
Customer Care Department within the United States at 800-762-2974, outside the United States at
317-572-3993 or fax 317-572-4002.

Wiley also publishes its books in a variety of electronic formats. Some content that appears in print may not
be available in electronic books.

For more information about Wiley products, visit our web site at www.wiley.com.

ISBN: 0-471-46061-3

Printed in the United States of America

10 9 8 7 6 5 4 3 2 1

Contents

1   The Cost of a College Education   1

Sticker Shock   1

The Rising Cost of College   6

How Much Will You Need To Save?   8

2   Where To Stash Your College Funds   15

Stocks   16

Bonds   18

Certificates of Deposit   22

U.S. Government Securities   23

Mutual Funds   25

3   Building a College Fund   29

Understanding Risk   29

Different Types of Risk   30

Allocating Your Investments   31

Setting Up Your Investments   35

4   Tuition Savings Plans   45

A New Twist on an Old Theme   46

The Drawbacks of 529 Savings Plans   49

Prepaid Plans   51

Savings Plans   60

5   Getting Professional Help   93

Who's Who in Financial Planning?   94

Fees and Service   96

Finding a Financial Planner   97

Smart Questions To Ask a Financial Planner   98

6   Reducing the Tab   101

Grants   104

Loans   105

Scholarships   105

Work-Study Programs   105

State Aid   106

Institutional Aid   106

Tax Breaks   107

College Tax Credits and Deductions   107

Smart Ways To Save   111

Getting Grandparents To Help   115

State Agencies   117

7   Applying for Financial Aid   123

The Different Types of Financial Aid   124

Are You Eligible for Aid?   124

Understanding the Financial Aid Forms   128

When Should You Apply?   130

Improving Your Aid Eligibility   132

How Does Financial Aid Work in Cases of Divorce?   136

Ask the Financial Aid Officer   137

Is the School Need Blind?   138

Negotiating a Better Package   138

8   The Search for Scholarship Money   141

The Search Begins   143

Show Me the Money   145

How To Apply for a Scholarship   150

A Scholarship Sampling   152

9   Smart Borrowing   159

Federal Loans   161

Subsidized versus Unsubsidized   162

Parent Loans for Undergraduate Students (PLUS)   163

State Loans   168

Private, or Alternative, Loans   168

Borrow from Yourself   172

Borrowing against Your Home   173

Refinancing Your Home Mortgage   174

Loans against a Life Insurance Policy   174

Loans from Retirement Plans   176

Borrowing against Stocks and Bonds   177

Personal Loans   178

Glossary   179

Index   183

CHAPTER 1

The Cost of a College Education

The cost of college is staggering. A four-year stint at a private college—and we are not even talking Princeton or Harvard here—will run you about $100,000 these days. If your youngster is just entering middle school, it will cost you 50 percent more—roughly $150,000—to send that kid off to a private university when he is ready. Your future Joe College is still in diapers? Expect to pay a whopping $245,000 by the time he steps foot on campus.

Grab your smelling salts, folks. College *is* expensive. The good news, though, is that this financial picture is not as bleak as it may seem. First, those figures that were cited previously include not just tuition, but room and board, books and supplies, transportation, and some personal expenses like shampoo, haircuts, and laundry. Second, public colleges charge slightly less than half those costs for residents: $45,000 this year and an estimated $113,000 in 18 years. Finally, very few parents will actually pay a college's full sticker price. Like passengers on an airplane, most college students will pay different prices—depending on the amount of financial aid or scholarships they receive—for their seats in the classroom.

Sticker Shock

How much will it really cost? There is tuition, of course. In addition, students need money for room and board (no, it is not included in the price of tuition),

1

books, supplies, telephone calls, laundry, and transportation to and from school. When you have added those costs, throw in another $2,000 to $3,000 per year for pizza money. Pizza money? That covers all those $50 and $75 checks that parents periodically send to their college student throughout the year, says Raymond D. Loewe, a chartered financial consultant and the president of College Money, a college planning firm in Marlton, NJ. The money pays for haircuts, toiletries, and prescriptions, and, well, those late-night pizzas when you are cramming for a test. Even though they are relatively small dollar amounts, those pizza checks can really add up over a year's time.

Once you have figured out the annual cost, multiply that number by four— or in a growing number of cases, five—for every year that your child will attend college. Then, multiply the results *again* by the number of students in the family. Vavoom! Suddenly, those initial numbers have mushroomed into an enormous amount, which is probably more than most families pay for their homes. College tuition is probably the largest expense, says Loewe, that most families will pay for *anything*.

Colleges today are loosely ranked into a three-tiered system:

- Public (or state) colleges
- Private colleges
- Ivy League-type schools

Public colleges—that is, schools supported by state and local governments —typically charge less than private colleges. However, if your child crosses your home state line and attends a college in another state, you will pay a higher, out-of-state tuition rate. Among public colleges, there is generally a big difference between the price of a two-year college and the price of a four-year college. Public two-year colleges (or community colleges) are generally less expensive. Four-year colleges, however, charge very different amounts, too. The U.S. Department of Education, in its "Managing the Price of College" booklet, groups *states*—as lower-priced, medium-priced, or higher-priced-based on the state's average tuition and the size of the state's student aid programs as shown:

LOWER-PRICED	MEDIUM-PRICED	HIGHER-PRICED
Arizona	Alabama	Connecticut
Arkansas	Alaska	Delaware
District of Columbia	California	Maine
Florida	Colorado	Maryland
Georgia	Illinois	Massachusetts

LOWER-PRICED	MEDIUM-PRICED	HIGHER-PRICED
Hawaii	Indiana	Michigan
Idaho	Iowa	New Hampshire
Kentucky	Kansas	New Jersey
Louisiana	Minnesota	Nevada
New Mexico	Mississippi	Ohio
North Carolina	Missouri	Pennsylvania
Oklahoma	Montana	Rhode Island
Tennessee	Nebraska	South Carolina
Texas	New York	Vermont
West Virginia	North Dakota	Virginia
Wyoming	South Dakota	
	Utah	
	Washington	
	Wisconsin	

Parents, of course, often look at these classifications differently, says Raymond Loewe. They rank the choices as expensive colleges, very expensive colleges, and absolutely ridiculously priced colleges!

But seriously, folks, are you ready now for some really good news? The sticker price of a college education works much like the sticker price on an automobile. Everyone talks about how expensive it is, but few people actually pay the full price. It all depends on the deal that you cut. Here is how it works: First, the cost of attendance may be reduced if your child qualifies for need-based financial aid and/or scholarships and grants. Secondly—and this is very important because it applies to most families—unless your family has a very high income, you probably will not be expected to pay the full price. Instead, you will be asked to pay a reduced amount, called your Expected Family Contribution (EFC). This is the dollar amount that you are expected to pay, based on your family's financial income and assets. (You can estimate your EFC with an online calculator at *www.finaid.org* or at *www.collegeboard.com*. Full details about your EFC and how it is calculated are discussed in Chapter 7.) If your son's education costs total $25,000 per year, for example, and your EFC is $15,000 per year, then a four-year-stay at the college should cost you just $60,000 (4 × $15,000). That is far less than the advertised sticker price! What about the remaining

$10,000 per year, though, that is not covered? That cost should be paid for through financial aid, such as student loans, scholarships, grants, and work-study programs—if the financial aid system works as it should. (It does not always, of course. See Chapter 7 for a complete explanation.) Thus, the best place to start when trying to assess the cost of college is your EFC. No matter what the school's official sticker price is, your EFC is the single best indicator of how much college will really cost your particular family.

Here is a sample breakdown (and explanation) of the average college costs —per year—that you can currently expect to pay at a four-year college, from the College Board in New York City. If your child will attend an out-of-state public school, expect to pay an average of $10,428 per year instead of the $4,081 figure listed in Table 1.1.

TABLE 1.1   The Bill . . . if Your Child Is Heading off to College Tomorrow

	PUBLIC	**PRIVATE**
Tuition and fees	$4,081	$18,273
Room and board	$5,582	$6,779
Books and supplies	$786	$807
Personal expenses	$1,643	$1,173
Transportation	$749	$645
Total costs for one year	$12,841	$27,677

Source: "Sample Undergraduate Budgets (Average), 2002–2003 (Enrollment-Weighted)" *Trends in College Pricing 2002.* Copyright 2002 by College Entrance Examination Board and collegeboard.com. Reprinted with permission. All rights reserved.

Tuition and Fees

Tuition is the charge for instruction. Fees cover the services your college provides, such as the library, student activities, or health center.

Room—Where You Live

Most colleges offer a variety of on-campus housing including dorms, larger suites, or townhouses. They are usually assigned on a lottery basis, giving the upper-class students first pick. Some students choose to live off-campus in order to pool their expenses.

Board—Where You Eat

There are a variety of meal plans used by colleges. Some offer an all-you-can-eat system where you are allowed to go back for seconds or thirds for each meal.

Others use a point system. That is, you are given a certain amount of points for the semester that you use to buy your meals.

Books and Supplies

Every college student has to buy books, pens, notebooks, and other things. Some courses require more supplies than others. For example, if you enroll in an art class, you may need to buy brushes and paint.

Personal Expenses

Of course, you will have some personal expenses for such things as laundry, toiletries, recreation, stereo equipment, and inflatable chairs. This is an area in which you can certainly get thrifty.

Transportation

Students who commute daily have to absorb the costs of gas and parking or pay for public transportation. Living on campus does not mean you will not leave the school for the years that you attend. Students usually go home several times a year for holidays or on breaks.

Will the Cost of a College Education Continue To Rise? If So, at Such a High Rate?

To answer this question, we have to look at inflation. In the late 1980s, both public and private college costs increased annually by about 7 or 8 percent, well above the regular inflation rate. In recent years, tuition hikes have slowed to about 4 or 5 percent, but that is still higher than the regular inflation rate. Your first reaction may be that the cost of college cannot possibly keep going up. How high can they realistically go? Or, perhaps you have read in the paper or heard on the news that college inflation is decreasing. Those tuition sticker prices must come down, then, or at the very least, remain stable, right? Not exactly. Raymond Loewe believes that although many institutions have been trying to hold the line on costs, most college prices, nevertheless, will continue to rise faster than inflation (but not *as fast* as prices rose 10 years ago)—for the foreseeable future. Why? Loewe says there are several reasons:

- *A college education is worth it.* You cannot really calculate the return on a college education (as you do with other investments), but most people will agree that a good college education provides the student with an edge to get ahead in life. A good college education teaches students how to learn, for instance. It gives them a knowledge base, prepares them to adapt to a changing world, and teaches them how to communicate better. In addition, college graduates tend to have more confidence in life than their counterparts; college gives students a range of experiences that non-college graduates may not be exposed to. A college diploma generally leads to increased lifetime earnings. Finally, and perhaps most important, says Raymond Loewe, students develop a network of contacts at college that can be extremely valuable throughout the rest of their lives.

As long as parents continue to believe this idea that college is worth it, their desire to send their children to the better, more costly schools will continue to keep demand—and thus, prices—up. (This, in fact, may be the most important reason that costs will remain high.)

- *College is labor intensive.* It has not been as easy to apply technological advances and efficiencies to the college classroom as it has been to other industries. You still need a lot of people (as opposed to computers) to provide a quality college environment. You can computerize the card catalog in the library, for instance, but you cannot replace the librarians themselves with machines. People, as we know all too well, says Loewe, are more expensive than computers because you must pay them a salary, offer medical and retirement benefits, and provide a comfortable workload. (One professor, for instance, cannot teach 10 courses per semester.)

- *Uncle Sam lets you borrow the money easily.* A perfect example is the Parent Loan for Undergraduate Students (PLUS). This loan lets parents borrow 100 percent of the cost of college (minus any financial aid that the student might receive). When colleges see this unlimited amount of money floating on the horizon, says Loewe, they have very little incentive to reduce costs.

- *Selecting a college is an emotional issue.* Students must work hard these days to get accepted to the best colleges. Competition is fierce—even among the best and brightest students. Parents are proud of their children's ability, naturally, to get accepted into these venerable—and often, very expensive—institutions. The decision to go to one school or another, then, cannot be just about money, says Loewe. For some, sending your kid to a certain university is the ultimate status symbol. For others, sending your kid to a certain university is never questioned—no matter what the cost or the size of the parents' wallets—because a college education is the last real gift that those parents will bestow upon their child before he or she leaves home. Can you really expect parents to throw away the American Dream of a first-rate college education just because it costs a few more bucks each month? (Or so it seems.) Ultimately, parents are often under tremendous pressure to ante up some extra dollars to pay those tuition bills.

The Rising Cost of College

Table 1.2 projects the average costs for college expenses, including tuition, fees, books, room and board, transportation, and other costs in the United States, assuming a 5 percent annual increase in expenses.

TABLE 1.2 The Rising Costs of College

CHILD'S AGE	PUBLIC (IN-STATE)	PUBLIC (OUT-OF-STATE)	PRIVATE
Newborn	$117,607	$174,761	$258,761
1	$112,007	$166,439	$246,439
2	$106,673	$158,514	$234,704
3	$101,593	$150,965	$223,527
4	$96,756	$143,777	$212,883
5	$92,148	$136,930	$202,746
6	$87,760	$130,410	$193,091
7	$83,581	$124,200	$183,896
8	$79,601	$118,285	$175,139
9	$75,811	$112,653	$166,799
10	$72,201	$107,288	$158,857
11	$68,762	$102,179	$151,292
12	$65,488	$97,314	$144,088
13	$62,370	$92,680	$137,226
14	$59,400	$88,266	$130,692
15	$56,571	$84,063	$124,468
16	$53,877	$80,060	$118,541
17	$51,312	$76,248	$112,896
18	$48,868	$72,617	$107,520

Source: *Based* on actual data reported by the College Board from "Annual Survey of Colleges" in *Trends in College Pricing, 1999.* Copyright 2001 by College Entrance Examination Board and collegeboard.com. Reprinted with permission. All rights reserved.

Do Your Homework

Do not rely on these general charts to estimate the cost of college. Instead, call the colleges that your child is interested in directly. Ask for the estimated total cost of education in the year that your child will attend. (Does the amount include just tuition, or most other costs, too, such as room and board and supplies?) Ask how much the school expects costs to increase each year. Most schools can provide you with this information. You can also find such data in a handbook such as *Barron's Profiles of American Colleges 2002, 25th Edition*. (This book will only give you current costs, however, not estimated future costs.) You may find that the private school you are interested in costs substantially less (or more) than the average figure cited in the previous table. To give you an idea of the variety of prices out there, look at the tabs cited in the following. Please note: The tuition is *per year*. At the public universities, resident prices/non-resident prices are listed. You will notice that these schools are a real bargain if you live in that particular state. Out-of-towners, though, are often expected to pay two or three times as much as residents. In some states, the rates for non-residents rival the cost of a private university! Also, the statistics on just tuition and room and board are given. The Barron's book (and other books like it that you will find in your bookstore or library) estimates costs for everything from books and supplies to transportation to personal expenses.

How Much Will You Need To Save?

Obviously, you will want to save as much as you can for college without sabotaging your other savings (for most folks, that is retirement savings, but it could be money you are setting aside to start a business or to buy a vacation home) and without sacrificing your lifestyle too much. You will have to cut back on some extras, but do not eliminate entirely those expenses that really bring joy to your family. Vacations, for example, are important to most families. Perhaps you will not spend three weeks in Europe this year. Or, if you do, perhaps you will stay at a lower-priced Bed & Breakfast instead of your usual luxury hotel.

However, how much is as much as you can? Are there any guidelines or formulas? There are formulas, yes—called college cost calculators—which can help you estimate how much you will need to save to send little Suzy to Yale in 10 years. Various web sites, such as *www.collegeboard.org*, and any of the mutual fund sites, such as *www.fidelity.com* or *www.troweprice.com*, have these calculators. Just type in some information about your child's age and the type of school he or she will attend (that is, public, private, or Ivy League), and the estimator will tell you how much you need to save. Before you click on any of those web sites, though, read this warning carefully: Those numbers are just *estimates,* and some of those estimates are ridiculously high. One web site that I visited, in fact, said I needed to save $900 per month if I hoped to send my three-year-old daughter to a good, private college someday. If you are gasping for air, imagine my response: I have two other school-age kids who are closer to college age than she is!

Regardless of what the estimates say, save as much as you can, using your EFC as a guideline. As flip as it sounds, it is the only realistic answer. For example, one calculator tells you to save $900 per month. Can you do that? Well, what can you do? $200 per month? $100? $50? Your options are not all or nothing. It is better to save something, no matter how small the amount. You can pay for the rest of the cost with loans, grants, scholarships, work-study programs, and some cost-cutting tactics (all of which are discussed in subsequent chapters).

If it makes you feel better, please understand that you are not alone. Most parents cannot—and do not save the entire amount needed for tuition, but they will not borrow it all either. Instead, they will pull the money from a variety of sources, namely: current income, savings, federal and state grants, college and private scholarships, work-study programs, and student and parent loans. The bottom line? You have four basic ways to pay for college, says Raymond Loewe:

- *Save the money*. Most parents do not save enough for college. No surprises there, right? Listen to this: Out of some 50,000 parents that Raymond Loewe has worked with over the years, less than 10—yes, 10—had saved enough money to pay the college bills.

  Some parents believe that either (a) they'll qualify for financial aid so they do not have to bother saving, or (b) that savings will just reduce the amount of financial aid that they will get so, in the long run, it does not pay to save. Unfortunately, both of these notions are erroneous. Here is why: Even if you do qualify for financial aid (and this is discussed in detail in Chapters 6 and 7), you will still need to pay some of that college tab. Financial aid does not cover everything. It is meant to fill in the gap, not give students a free ride. Most financial aid packages—even those for the neediest students—include loans that need to be paid back.

  And as far as savings reducing the amount of financial aid that you receive, forget about it. Financial aid formulas are heavily tilted toward income, not assets. The larger your income, the less likely you are to receive financial aid. Parental assets do play some part in the calculation, of course, but current income is the most heavily weighted factor. What is more, you will most likely need some savings just to meet your EFC. If you do not have any savings set aside for college, you may have to borrow just to meet your EFC.

- *The pay as you go plan*. This method works just as its name implies: You pay the tuition, as you go, from current income. The trouble is, you have to increase earnings sufficiently to cover the cost of the tuition *and* the cost of taxes that you have to pay on the extra income. If you need $10,000 per year for tuition, for example, you will need more than a salary hike of $10,000 per year. Why? Your income is taxed, remember, so your take home pay is less than your actual salary. (How much less depends on your tax bracket.)

  The other downside? This payment method can backfire if you qualify for aid. Financial aid is based largely on your family income (not your assets), earned in the *prior* year. Let us assume that your son is just entering college as a freshman. You filed for financial aid and were awarded a small aid package. It is not enough to cover your bill, though, so you decide to take on some consulting work this year to help pay the tab. Next year, your son applies for financial aid again—and this time, he gets even less! The reason: Your increased income has lowered your need for the subsequent year. As a result, your family must increase its income even more the second year to pay its bills, which means you will get even less financial aid the third year, and so on, and so on. A pay-as-you-go system appears to work well on paper, says Loewe, but it often does not do the job.

- *Borrow the money.* Whether your child takes out a student loan or you borrow against the house, your insurance policy, or your retirement plan, borrowing the money is a common way to get the cash needed for college. (Borrowing is discussed in detail in Chapter 9.) Although student loans are typically lower than commercial loans, you (or your child) must still pay this money back. That means young graduates will be saddled with loan repayments for years, or you will have to assume the debt just when you are probably thinking about retirement. Often, parents borrow far too much for college, says Loewe, because they simply have not saved enough, and the emotional issues of college—as in, "I want to give my daughter more opportunities than I had so I am sending her to an elite, private college" —cause parents to bite off more than they should.

- *Let someone else pick up the tab.* If wealthy grandparents are on the scene (with a checkbook ready, of course), congratulations. You do not have too much to worry about. However, for most folks, letting someone else pick up your kid's college bill usually means qualifying for financial aid. As you will see in Chapters 6 and 7 on financial aid, federal, state, and institutional aid is based on your financial need (which is determined by a formula), and it is not all *free.* Aid that is given in the form of low-cost loans must be paid back.

Time Is Your Best Resource

Start when you are young, and be consistent. That sage advice applies to an exercise regime, a healthy diet, saving for retirement, and, among other things, saving for your child's college education. If you start saving money for your children's college education when they are young, you will have more years to save—and more years for your money to earn interest. In the long run, you will generally need to save far less than last-minute savers. Why? Start saving when your child is still young and you will be able to take more investment risk (see Chapters 2 and 3 for details), which will often yield higher returns.

In addition, time lets your savings *compound.* (That is, interest or earnings build up not only on the original money invested but on the interest/earnings reinvested in previous years.) Over time, compounding is a mighty powerful tool. So powerful, in fact, that the more time you have for your money to grow, the less money (overall) you will actually have to set aside to achieve your investment goals (see Table 1.3). To accumulate $10,000 (after tax), you could save $144 per month for five years (assuming earnings of 8 percent per year). Total savings required: $8,640. Early birds could save the same amount, however, for far less money. You could accumulate that same $10,000 (assuming the same earnings of 8 percent) by saving $26 per month, for 18 years. The total savings required in this situation? Just $5,616.

At first glance, you may think that the difference isn't that remarkable. It is only $3,000 after all. But that is where you would be wrong. It is not just $3,000. It is $3,000 *per $10,000 accumulated*. Who is going to save just $10,000 for college? You are going to save 5 or 10 times that amount. (At least, you are going to try.) That $3,000 savings, then, is just the tip of the iceberg. Start saving early and you will have to sock away thousands less than if you get a late start.

Before you shake your head in dismay, however, understand that most parents do not follow this prescription. That is, they do *not* start saving for college when their child is still in diapers. Instead, they put it off and put it off until ... well, you fill in the blank. The best course of action is, naturally, to start saving when your kids are young. That will give you the most options. However, if you are late to the college savings game, then it is time to make tracks. You cannot procrastinate any longer. If your current budget is tight, and you can only squeeze out $50 per month, then start with that amount. Any amount of savings is better than none. The key is to get started. The sooner you start saving, the better.

Once you start saving, you should keep on saving without fail. (That should be the plan anyway.) You will put a certain amount away each month or year and take advantage of dollar cost averaging. (When you regularly invest a fixed amount in a stock or mutual fund—no matter if the market goes up or down—your average purchase price is lower than the average market price over the

TABLE 1.3 Monthly Savings Needed To Accumulate $10,000

EARNINGS RATE (BEFORE TAXES)	5 YEARS	10 YEARS	18 YEARS
4%	$155	$72	$35
6%	$150	$67	$31
8%	$144	$62	$26
10%	$139	$57	$23

same time period. That is dollar cost averaging.) Unfortunately, things may not work out as planned. Some years you may have to spend extra for remedial tutoring or braces; other years you may earn a bigger bonus at work or a larger refund from the IRS. The key, again, is just to put some money away. If you can do it regularly, great. Once you get started—and see the results of your efforts —you may be encouraged (much as you would be with a weight loss program) to keep it up or even to save more. However, if you find it easier to save in a lump sum periodically, that can prove effective over the long run, too. To give you an idea of how these two styles stack up financially, notice the chart from the Mutual Fund Education Alliance (see Table 1.4).

Of course, scraping the money together is just one part of the college savings equation. Next, you have to decide how to invest the money that you have set

TABLE 1.4 Monthly Investments versus Lump-Sum Investments**

	MONTHLY INVESTMENTS		
YEARS TO INVEST	**$50**	**$200**	**$500**
3	$2,027	$8,107	$20,268
6	4,601	18,405	46,013
9	7,871	31,486	78,715
12	12,025	48,102	120,254
15	17,302	69,208	173,019
18	24,004	96,017	240,043
	LUMP-SUM INVESTMENT		
YEARS TO INVEST	**$10,000**	**$25,000**	**$50,000**
3	$12,597	$31,493	$62,986
6	15,869	39,672	79,344
9	19,990	49,975	99,950
12	25,182	62,954	125,908
15	31,722	79,304	156,608
18	39,960	99,900	199,801

** These figures assume an 8 percent yield compounded annually.

aside for college. Most average, middle-of-the-road investments (not pork bellies or gold futures here) will help your money grow over the years, but, depending on how far away that first tuition bills is, some investments will better suit your needs than others. If you trust your savings to investments that are too conservative—especially when your child is very young, for example—you run the risk that your investment will not keep up with inflation and taxes. Plunk those dollars into a vehicle that is too risky, though—especially when your child is nearing college age—and you could risk losing some of those hard-earned savings. Your savings should be invested so they reap the biggest return (with an acceptable amount of risk), within the time frame that you have. In Chapters 2 and 3, you will learn about different types of investments that will work for you —now and when your child gets closer to college age. You will also learn in whose name the money should be invested and how savings affect your chances of getting financial aid.

CHAPTER 2

Where To Stash Your College Funds

Whether your child is 15 years away from college—or just 2 years shy of the big event—you must think about where you would like to stash your savings. What types of savings or investments, for instance, are appropriate for education funding? Stocks? Bonds? Mutual funds? Then, you must consider how you will set up those investments. Do you want to set up a custodial account for your child, or are you interested in a Coverdell education tuition savings plans?

The types of investments that you choose will depend, in large part, on your *timing*. Typically, the investments that you pick when your son is a toddler will probably not be appropriate when he reaches high school age (or at least not in the same proportions). Why? If you need the funds earmarked for college in 2 or 3 years, let us say, you generally cannot afford as much investment risk as you might have taken 10 years earlier. In most cases, that will mean that you will need a safer investment such as a short-term bond fund or a certificate of deposit. Picking the appropriate investment vehicle poses a host of other issues. If you go the custodial account route, for example, you will eventually have to hand over control of the funds to your child. Will you feel comfortable doing that? If you pick a state-sponsored savings plan, however, you will give up control of how your assets are allocated over time. Will you feel comfortable doing *that*?

All of these issues will come into play as you develop a college fund investment strategy. Before we actually sit down and start to figure out how to build a college fund (which we will do in the next chapter), let us look first at the building materials themselves: the various types of investments that are available and are appropriate for college savings.

Stocks

Stocks are one of the most common types of investments, and they offer one of the best opportunities for long-term growth. Based on historic averages, only stocks, in fact, have continuously outpaced inflation and generated double-digit returns. Consider this: If you invest $1,200 every year in stocks—and you earn a constant 10 percent return—you will have $60,191 in 18 years. Not too shabby, eh? That makes stocks a good choice for building a college savings fund. Most investors, in fact—yes, even the most conservative investors among us—should allocate at least a portion of their college savings to stocks.

The higher yield that you historically get with stocks comes with a price, of course. It is a higher degree of risk. Because stock prices go up and down—that is all the talk that you hear in the news, by the way, about this company's stock up a point and that company's stock down two points—there is a greater chance that you could lose money. You can reduce this risk of a stock's short-term volatility by investing in stocks for *the long term*. In most cases, that means you can invest money in stocks—and not lose sleep over it—if you do not need that investment cash for at least three to five years. The reasoning: Stock prices go up and down. If you need to sell your shares when the market is down, you will lose money. If you have time to weather the ups and downs of the market, you can wait out a market downturn and sell your shares when the market is up again. When held for long periods of time, stock investments have consistently outperformed other investments.

You can also lessen your risk with stocks by spreading your money among different types of stocks and other, less-volatile investments such as bonds. For high-speed performance, you will want small-cap or growth stocks. Want less risk, even if it means you will have to settle for less spectacular growth? You do not have to rule out stocks entirely. Instead, invest in steadier (but slower-growing) blue chip stocks or an index fund, which invests in companies that make up a particular index such as the Standard & Poor's (S&P) 500. Index funds do not try to beat the market, just match it. As dull as that investing strategy may sound, index funds are often a good choice for investors (especially novice investors) because they mirror the market's overall performance. That is not bad when you consider that less than a third of stock funds actually outperform the S&P 500 each year.

In general, most financial experts believe that it is better for the average investor to invest in a stock mutual fund rather than individual stocks because funds offer diversification and professional management. You can invest $2,000 in a mutual fund, for example, and reap the same rate of return as someone who invests $20,000. Your risk is reduced, too, because the mutual fund's assets are invested not in one stock, but in many different stocks. It would take a lot of money to buy the kind of diversification that you get with mutual funds in individual stocks.

When you invest in stocks, you can make money in two basic ways:

- The company is profitable (or is expected to become profitable). As a result, its stock price may rise in value, producing a *capital gain* when you sell your shares. At that time you will earn a profit by selling your shares for a higher price than you paid for them. The gain is the difference between the price you paid for the stock and the price at which you ultimately sold the stock.

- Some companies share some of the firm's profits with shareholders. These cash payments, called *dividends,* are paid to shareholders quarterly or twice each year. (Not all stocks pay dividends. Some companies, especially young, fast-growing companies, channel the profits back into the company to help fuel the company's fast growth.)

A STOCK PRIMER

A share of stock represents partial ownership of a company. When you buy stock shares, it is like you are buying a tiny piece of the company. If you own shares of Microsoft stock, for example, you are a part owner with Microsoft founder and majority-owner Bill Gates, along with the thousands of other investors who also own Microsoft stock. A stock is often called an *equity investment* because you are buying ownership, or equity, in the company.

Stocks are categorized in several different ways. One way to classify stocks, for instance, is by *size*: small, medium, or large. Large company stocks generally provide more stability, whereas small company stocks are generally riskier, but provide more opportunity for faster growth. Some large company stocks are referred to as *blue chips*. Although there is no hard and fast rule that defines a blue chip, these are stocks of large companies that, over the years, have provided steady growth and reliable dividends. In any portfolio invested for the long term, you should typically find some money invested in blue chip stocks.

Another way to classify stocks is by *growth*. Aggressive growth, for example, usually applies to smaller companies that are expected to grow faster than average. Because there is more risk that these companies might drop precipitously in value, you expect to earn a higher return with these stocks. *Growth-and-income* refers to older, more established companies that are not growing quite so fast (and are thus less volatile). These types of stocks generally do not have the potential to offer the soaring returns of aggressive growth stocks. However they are also not as risky. When the market experiences a downturn, these stocks may fall, but generally not as hard as faster-growing stocks. In addition, growth-and-income stocks usually pay dividends.

You can also classify stocks as domestic or international. Domestic stocks are simply the stocks of companies that are based in the United States. International stocks, meanwhile, are stocks of companies that are based outside the United States. Domestic stocks generally provide more stability. International stocks generally provide more opportunity for growth (but again, are riskier). International stocks are often further divided into two broad categories: developed countries and emerging markets. Developed countries are those free market economies outside the United States, which, obviously, are fully developed. The emerging markets refer to countries, such as India and Malaysia, which are still developing. These stocks tend to be more volatile than domestic or even other international stocks. It is not unusual for emerging market investments to increase or decrease 30 percent or more during a given year.

Bonds

When a company, the government, or a municipality issues a bond, it is basically writing an IOU to raise money. You lend money to the issuer by making an investment in a bond. In return, you are repaid with a fixed rate of interest. (In most cases, you receive regular interest payments.) At maturity, you receive your principal (the original amount invested). Bonds are commonly referred to as *fixed income* investments because they typically pay interest to bondholders on a regular, or fixed basis.

Some investors believe that bonds are a good, stable college investment because you know exactly how much your investment will be worth when the bond matures. At first glance, it looks like a sure thing. If you need $30,000 in 15 years, for example, then you must buy enough bonds today that will pay that amount upon maturity after featuring in the interest collected over these years.

The trouble with bonds, though, is that historically, they have not matched the long-term return of stocks. Some bonds, in fact, will earn barely enough to keep pace with college inflation. As we will see in the next chapter, there is certainly a place for bonds in your college portfolio. Bonds can be used to diversify a portfolio, for example, because they balance out the ups and downs of the stock portion. Bonds provide a steady stream of income and they are also often excellent, lower-risk investment vehicles for the *short term*, as in less than five years. However, bonds alone will not provide the high growth that you need, especially if your future college student is currently still in diapers.

Also, bonds are not exactly the risk-free investment that some people assume. The risk with bonds, in fact, is twofold. The company or government agency that issued the bond could *default.* That is, they cannot pay interest or repay your principal. You can minimize this risk by checking the bond issuer's creditworthiness, investing in only high-quality rather than junk or high-yield-bonds, and investing in a bond fund rather than just a single bond. Like a stock mutual fund, a bond mutual fund lowers your risk because it invests your money in many bonds. If one bond defaults, you will not lose all of your money.

The other risk is that unless you hold a bond until maturity, you risk losing some of your principal. Here is how it works: Bonds have an inverse relationship with interest rates. If interest rates have risen since your bond was issued, your bond will be worth less than it was when you bought it. Let us look at an example: The bond that you bought five years ago is paying 5 percent interest. Your bond does not mature for another 5 years, but you are short on cash, so you decide to sell the bond early. Interest rates have gone up, though, and newly issued bonds are now offering a 6 percent interest rate. Who will want to buy your bond, then, if they can buy a new bond that pays a higher interest rate? That is the problem. To attract a buyer, the price of the bond must be reduced to compensate for the lower interest rate. In effect, the price must be low enough so that the buyer of your bond will get the same return as he would have gotten with a new bond. This is commonly referred to as *selling at a discount*.

In addition, the longer a bond's maturity, the farther the price will drop (as interest rates rise). That is why you will often hear that long-term bonds are a riskier investment than short-term bonds.

Conversely, if interest rates have fallen, your bond will be worth more. Why? Your bond is still paying that 5 percent interest. However, this time, interest rates have fallen. Newly issued bonds are now paying just 4 percent interest. When you sell before maturity, buyers will pay more for your bond because your bond has a higher interest rate. This is commonly referred to as *selling at a premium*.

The risk that you will have to reduce or raise the price of your bond will not affect you, of course, if you plan to hold your bond until maturity. However, if you want to sell ahead of time, it does, or if you invest in a mutual fund that trades bonds. (Keep in mind: Many people *plan* on holding the bonds they purchase until maturity. However, for one reason or another, they often find themselves selling them before maturity.)

At maturity, you will generally be repaid the bond's full value *unless* the bond issuer defaults. Or, the bond is *called*. This happens when the issuer pays off the bond before it is due. You will still get your full investment principal back, but you might not receive as much income interest as you had expected.

Like stocks, you can buy bonds individually or in a mutual fund. There is some disagreement as to which is the best way to buy bonds. The answer depends on how much money you have to invest in bonds and the types of bonds that you are thinking of buying. Bond funds offer diversity (which spreads out your risk). Often, it is tough to buy that diversity with individual bonds unless you have a lot of money to invest. The downside: Unlike individual bonds, bond mutual funds do not promise a fixed interest income, and they do not guarantee that your principal will be returned. Because a bond fund is traded continuously by a fund manager, it acts more like a stock mutual fund than an individual bond.

Whether you should by a fund or an individual bond also depends on the type of bond that you want. If you are buying a Treasury bond, for example, get it yourself. They are super-safe, and you can buy it commission-free from Treasury Direct (see the *Buying Investments* section at the end of this chapter). You are not gaining anything when you buy Treasuries in a fund. If you want municipal, corporate, or junk bonds, though, you are probably better off with a fund. Why?

A BOND PRIMER

All bonds have *maturity* dates, and these dates impact its current value. Typically, bonds are paid off at maturity. That is, on that date the amount borrowed (called the *principal*) must be paid back to you. Bonds are issued in a wide range of maturities. Short-term bonds mature in three years or less. Intermediate-term bonds mature in 3 to 10 years. Long-term bonds mature in 10 years or more.

Bonds are graded according to their *creditworthiness* by rating agencies. What determines creditworthiness? The issuer's ability to pay interest on the bond and repay your principal when the bond matures. Companies or government agencies that are more likely to default—and *not* make those payments—are awarded lower ratings.

Two of the most common rating agencies are Moody's Investors Service and S&P. These services assign letter grades to indicate a bond's creditworthiness. A highly speculative bond, for example, is graded a CC by S&P and a Ca by Moody's; a high quality bond is graded an AA by S&P and an Aa by Moody's.

A bond's value will also depend on who issued it. U.S. Treasury bonds, bills, and notes, for example, are issued by the federal government. These securities are super-safe because they are backed by the full faith and credit of the federal government.

Municipal bonds, commonly referred to as *munis,* are sold by state and local governments. You do not pay any federal tax on the interest you earn from a muni. You may not pay state taxes on muni interest either, depending on your state's law. Because of these tax-exempt features, munis pay a lower interest rate than other bonds. Maturities for municipal bonds range from one year to about 35 years. Because of the tax savings, investors in high-tax brackets often buy munis.

Corporate bonds, which are sold by companies, generally pay higher interest rates than other bonds because there is a greater chance that a company will default on its bond payments than the government will. (However, it is not too likely that a big, well-established company will default on its bonds.) A high-yield, or *junk*, bond is a corporate bond that pays an even higher interest rate. Why? It is issued by a company with a low credit rating and is at greater risk of default.

You need a minimum of $5,000 to invest in most munis and corporate bonds, and junk bonds are just too risky to invest in on an individual basis. A junk bond fund will cushion the volatility of these high-yield bonds.

Baccalaureate bonds are a type of municipal bond sold by some states especially for college savings. They come in maturities ranging from 5 to 21 years. Their main attractions are that they are exempt from federal income taxes, and if you live in the state issuing the bond, they are exempt from state and local taxes, too. As with other bonds, buy a baccalaureate bond that will mature when you need it. If you have to cash in early, you could take a loss.

The interest that the bond issuer agrees to pay you is based on the bond's *coupon rate*. This coupon rate depends on two factors:

- *The creditworthiness of the bond's issuer.* Bonds with lower investment ratings typically pay higher interest rates than bonds with stronger ratings.
- *The length of maturity.* The longer the maturity of the bond, the higher the bond's interest rate. Why? Most investors require a higher interest rate to compensate them for not having access to their money for a longer period of time.

WHAT ABOUT LIFE INSURANCE?

Cash-value life insurance policies, which include whole life, universal life, and variable life, offer a savings feature as well as the traditional insurance coverage. That is, part of your premium is *invested*. (Term life insurance has no cash value, so it does not figure into this picture.) Some agents tout these policies as good long-term saving vehicles because your money grows on a tax-deferred basis. The tax-deferred bit is true, but whether they make good long-term investments for college is debatable.

First, up-front commissions are steep, so unless you plan on keeping the policy for 10 years or more, you will not make up the cost of those early fees. Second, most folks would do better investing their money in other tax-deferred vehicles such as an IRA or a 401(k) plan. Why? You get the same tax advantages without the added cost of the insurance policy. You also have so many more investment options. Whole life and universal life typically invest in bonds and more conservative investments, for example, which probably will not generate the kind of returns that you need to build a college fund. Most variable universal life policies, though, do offer several mutual fund investment options, including some stock funds. (If you are going to invest in a policy, a variable universal policy is probably your best choice.) The bottom line: A cash-value life insurance policy may have some merit for long-term savings if you need insurance anyway, and you have enough cash to pay the premiums *and* stash additional money for college in other investments.

Certificates of Deposit

With a Certificate of Deposit (CD), you deposit a set amount of money—often $500 or more—and you are guaranteed a stated interest rate at the end of the period. CDs come in a range of maturities: 1, 2, 3, 6, and 12 months and 2 to 10 years. The longer that you agree to invest your money—and often, the more money that you invest—the higher your interest rate will be.

The interest rate paid on CDs varies from one bank to another, so it often pays to shop around. By all means, check out your local bank, but do not overlook those top-yielding rates offered at out-of-town banks. (CDs are federally insured up to FDIC limits, so it is equally safe to invest in the neighborhood bank as it is with a bank across the country.) Look in the *Wall Street Journal* or even your daily newspaper for a list of top-yielding CDs nationwide. Check out these web sites for listings, too: Rate.net (*www.rate.net*) and the bankrate.com (*www.bankrate.com*).

CDs are very low-risk investments that generally do not keep pace with college inflation. They do *not* offer the kinds of returns that most parents need to accumulate money for college. That means, they are not good long-term investments. However, CDs can be excellent places to park college savings that you will need in the immediate future (and do not want to risk losing).

You will have to make sure that you time your CDs right, though. If you need the money to pay tuition in September, for example, make sure that your CD matures in late August. Otherwise, you will be charged a penalty—often it can be as much as six month's worth of interest—if you withdraw the money before your CD matures.

There is a special CD designed specifically for college savings. Called the *CollegeSure CD*, it is offered by the College Savings Bank of Princeton, New Jersey. It is a CD indexed to college costs. Each year, your money always earns interest at a rate at least equal to the rise in college costs. What if there are years when college inflation is low? You do have the protection of a floor rate. This CD guarantees that you will earn, at the very least, 3 percent each year.

Principal and interest are FDIC insured—that is, backed up to $100,000 per depositor. In addition, the CollegeSure CD is guaranteed to meet future tuition, fees, room, and board, no matter how high those costs climb. Here is how it works:

CollegeSure CDs are available in maturities from 1 to 25 years, so you can time your CDs to mature when your child is ready to attend college. Each CD is sold in units or fractions of units. Upon maturity, one full unit, for example, is equal to one full year's cost for tuition, fees, room, and board at the average four-year private college. A fractional unit of 0.40 is equal to one year at the average in-state, public college. In other words, the amount of college you prepay today (one year of private college, for example) is guaranteed to be the same amount of college you will receive when your CollegeSure CDs mature. Ultimately, you must buy enough units to cover your child's college costs when he or she is ready to head off to campus. If your child decides not to go to college when the CD matures, there is no penalty per se: You simply get your investment back, plus the interest earned.

Investing in this type of CD is easier and more flexible than a typical bank CD. You can open an account with $500. There are no fees for this investment. Once this CD matures, you can use the principal and accumulated interest at any school.

Like other CDs, the CollegeSure CD is a taxable account. You can also invest in a CollegeSure CD through a tax-advantaged college savings program such as a 529 plan. (See the state of Montana's and the state of Arizona's 529 plans in Chapter 4.) For additional information about CollegeSure CDs, contact the College Savings Bank, 5 Vaughn Drive, Princeton, NJ 08540, 800-888-2723, *www.collegesavings.com*, e-mail to info@collegesavings.com.

U.S. Government Securities

Series EE bonds, commonly known as *savings bonds*, are guaranteed by the full faith and credit of the U.S. Treasury. You buy these bonds for half their face value, which can be $50, $75, $100, $500, $1,000, $5,000, or $10,000. A $100 bond, for example, costs $50. Over time, the value of the bond increases. When you cash in that bond at the final maturity date (30 years after purchase), for example, it will be worth $100, $200 or more depending on interest rates.

Series I bonds are sold in the same denominations as EE bonds but at face value—you pay $100 for a $100 bond. Interest rates on I bonds may be higher or lower than rates on EE bonds (the rates are adjusted every six months). The interest on I bonds can also be deferred until redemption or maturity.

Interest on savings bonds is exempt from state and local taxes. You can defer paying federal tax on these bonds until you cash them in. You may not have to pay any tax at all on these bonds, however, if you bought the bonds after 1990, and you ultimately use the bonds to pay for your child's college education. Unfortunately, that deal is not nearly as good as it sounds. "There are too many rules. And no big benefits," says Robert Doyle, a CPA and a personal financial specialist with Spoor Doyle & Associates in St. Petersburg, Florida. "It's an antiquated investment." Here is why, he says:

- To qualify for the tax-free interest, you must use the money for tuition only. Other college-related expenses, such as room, board, and books, do not qualify.
- The bond has to be in the parent's name, not the child's, to qualify. How often does that happen? Not as much as you might think. People often buy

savings bonds as gifts for newborns or children. In this case, the bonds are almost always given in the child's name.

- To qualify for a full exemption in 2003, your adjusted gross income cannot exceed $87,750 if you are married and filing a joint return. The tax exemption phases out completely if you and your spouse have a joint income of $117,750 or more.

Even if your knowledge of investing and the stock market is rather limited, you have probably heard of *T-bills*. T-bills, or U.S. Treasury Bills, are often cited as a benchmark for other investments. Why is that? Because Treasury securities have what is called the full faith and credit of the U.S. government behind them; they are super-safe investments. You *cannot* lose your money as long as you do not sell your T-bill before maturity. When making decisions about other investments that involve more risk, it is helpful to see how those investments performed in comparison to zero-risk T-bills. Investments that involve more risk should yield higher returns. Thus, you should ask yourself: How much higher is the return on the riskier investments? Is that anticipated return worth the added risk?

There are three major classes of Treasury securities: T-bills, T-notes, and T-bonds. With all three varieties, you are basically lending Uncle Sam money (that is the amount you invest in the bill, note, or bond) for a stated time period. In return, you receive interest, and when the bill or note matures, you get your principal back. These three Treasury securities differ mainly in terms of investment amount and the length of maturity. You can buy T-bills, for example, in minimum denominations of $10,000. These securities are issued with the shortest maturities: 1-month, 3-month and 6-month maturities. You buy a T-bill at a discount from its face value. You do not receive any interest while you hold the T-bill. At maturity, you cash the T-bill in for the face value. The interest that you earn on a T-bill is the difference between the discount purchase price and the maturity value. T-notes and T-bonds work a bit differently. You receive interest on these securities every six months. T-notes are sold in 2-year to 10-year maturities. The minimum investment amount is $5,000. (If you buy a note for 4 years or longer, the minimum drops to $1,000.) T-bonds, which have a maturity of 10 years, require a $1,000 minimum investment. With all three types of Treasury securities, you will owe federal tax on the interest earned, but you are exempt from state and local taxes.

In terms of college savings, many investors use T-bills and T-notes as a safe parking place for money that they will need *soon* to pay tuition bills. The interest earned on these types of investments is not enough, however, for money invested long term. That is why T-bonds should not be on your radar screen. If you have 10 years until your son or daughter goes off to college, you need a higher-yielding investment that will let you accumulate the amount of funds you need. Over a 10-year period, remember, you can handle a bit more risk because you have time to weather the ups and downs of the market.

Zero-coupon Treasury bonds are sold for substantially less than their face value. They do not pay any interest until maturity; instead, interest gets reinvested automatically. A $1,000 zero-coupon bond may sell for $500, for example, and be redeemed 10 years later for the full value. What troubles some investors about this type of bond, however, is that, although you do not receive any money until the bond matures, you must pay tax on the interest earned each year as though you had actually received it. Essentially, you are prepaying taxes on money that you will get in the future. Because of this tax, some people like to buy zero coupon bonds in a child's name because the child will pay less tax on them. You can buy zero-coupon bonds from securities firms, discount brokers, and local banks.

Mutual Funds

Rather than buying stocks, bonds, or money market securities on your own, a mutual fund lets you pool your investment money with other investors. The mutual fund then takes that money and invests it—under the guidance of a professional money manager—in a variety of stocks, bonds, or other securities. Each investor owns shares in that investment portfolio, which in turn owns shares in many companies. That means your investment is automatically diversified! If you were investing on your own, you probably could not afford to invest in such a wide variety of stocks and/or bonds.

Most mutual funds require a minimum investment of $1,000 or more, but many funds waive that requirement if you sign up to have money automatically transferred from your checking account to the fund every month. What is more, mutual funds appeal to most investors because there are so many different types of mutual funds to pick from. You can choose from lower-risk money market mutual funds to more moderate-risk balanced funds (which invest in both stocks and bonds) to higher-risk aggressive growth stock funds. Some other choices include:

- *International funds*, which invest in stocks of foreign companies
- *Global funds*, which invest in stocks of companies all over the world (including the United States)
- *Sector funds*, which invest in the stocks of one particular industry, such as the computer or healthcare industry
- *Index funds*, which invest in the stocks of companies that make up an index such as the S&P 500 Stock Index

Like bank money market accounts, *Money Market Mutual Funds* invest primarily in short-term, safe investments such as T-bills and CDs. There is very little risk to your money. (However, unlike a bank money market account, these funds are not FDIC-insured.) In addition, these funds pay interest monthly, and you get check-writing privileges. That makes them a popular choice for college money needed *now* because you can write checks directly from the account to your child's school. Generally, these mutual funds pay a little more in interest than similar bank money market accounts.

A MUTUAL FUND PRIMER

Mutual funds are classified as either *load* or *no-load* funds. Load funds charge you a sales fee, or load, to compensate the person who sold the fund to you. A typical load is 3 to 8 percent of your investment. A no-load fund does not charge a sales fee. About half of the funds available today are no-load funds. These funds are purchased directly by investors from the mutual fund company, such as Fidelity or Vanguard, without the assistance of a broker.

Mutual funds may also charge 12b-1 fees. Like a sales load, these costs may be used to compensate the selling broker. They are also used to pay for advertising and other costs of promoting the fund to investors. Even if a fund is advertised as a no load fund, it may still charge a small 12b-1 fee. You will never see 12b-1 fees deducted from your account. Instead, they are built into the cost of running the mutual fund and will simply reduce the amount of your fund's return.

How do you actually pick a fund? Before investing, check out the following key factors:

- Find out what the fund invests in. Obviously, the type of assets that a fund invests in, such as stocks, bonds, or U.S. Treasuries, will affect your investment return. An aggressive growth stock fund, for example, will offer a higher return — and a higher level of risk — than a U.S. government bond fund.
  - *Consider the fund's past performance.* Look at the fund's 3-, 5-, and 10-year returns. What are you looking for? Ideally, you want to see steady growth over many years rather than one or two sensational years sandwiched between several mediocre or poor years.
  - *Ask about the portfolio manager.* The portfolio manager works for the fund and is responsible for the fund's daily investment activities. Has the portfolio manager been running the fund for several years, or is he or she new to the fund? In some cases, the answer may affect the stability and future growth of the fund.
  - *Check out the costs.* In addition to sales loads and 12b-1 fees, mutual funds also charge management fees ranging from 0.5 to 1.5 percent per year. The more you pay in fees, though, the higher your investment return must be to make up for this additional cost.

Note: You can get most of the previous information directly from the mutual fund company. Call and ask for a prospectus to be mailed to you or visit the fund's web site. For a more objective view, also check independent sources, such as Lipper Analytical or Morningstar, which rate most mutual funds' performance. In addition, most of the financial magazines, such as *Money, Kiplinger's,* and *BusinessWeek*, devote an issue annually to mutual funds.

Buying Investments

- *Treasury securities.* You can buy these from a bank or a broker, for a fee. To avoid paying that commission, you can buy T-notes, T-bills, and T-bonds directly from the Federal Reserve through a program called Treasury Direct (*www.publicdebt.treas.gov/sec/sectrdir.htm*). If you want to sell your Treasuries, you can use the sell direct program. Again, the government will act as your broker. With this transaction, though, you will be charged a small fee.

- *Stocks.* You can buy stocks directly through either a full-service or a discount broker. You can also buy stocks online.

- *Bonds.* For most bond transactions, you must use a broker. Find out if you have to pay a commission and/or transaction costs. (Often, these fees are built into the price of the bond.)

- *Mutual funds.* If you buy a fund through a broker, you will pay a sales commission. However, you can buy a no-load fund directly from a mutual fund company.

- *CDs.* You will find these types of investments at banks. There is no commissions or fees.

CHAPTER 3

Building a College Fund

College is like a car ride. For those of us who do not make preparations ahead of time—and especially for those of us with more than one child—it can be a very *loooong* trip. The first thing you have to do is figure out where you are going. Fortunately, that much we know already. The university is looming in the distance, but distance is the operative word here. Whether our trip is short (just one or two years) or long (your kid is still in diapers), you need a road map that will provide the most suitable route. Notice I did not say fastest, safest, or cheapest, but most suitable. Some of us like to take the scenic route after all, and some of us like to drive beyond the speed limit, straight through the night.

In this chapter, we are going to work on drawing up a suitable road map. To do that successfully, you need to first figure out what kind of driver you are. Are you willing to take some risks? Does a smooth, straight run sound downright boring, or does even the slightest bump make your head spin? Secondly, you need to think about the type of investments that you will take on this trip. Will you keep the same investments from start to finish or will you switch? If so, how frequently? What will you add? What will you eliminate? Lastly, you need to figure out if you actually want to do the driving during this investment trip. If you feel more comfortable in the back seat (barking out occasional directions), you can turn the wheel over to someone else.

Understanding Risk

Whether you invest in stocks, bonds, or certificates of deposit (CDs), you might lose some (or all) of the money that you have invested. That is the risk you take in exchange for the opportunity for your money to grow. How much risk should you take, though, with a college fund? That depends on several factors.

First, figure out when you need the money. That is called your *time horizon.* When building a college fund, your time horizon is determined by the number of years until your child reaches college age. If your daughter is now two years old, for example, that means you have a time horizon of roughly 16 years. Why roughly? Does not 18 (the age at which most kids go to college) minus two (the age used in the previous example) equal 16 *exactly*? Yes, but the college investment time horizon does not end precisely at high school graduation. You certainly need *some* money at that point, as in the first year's tuition payments, but you certainly do not need all of it. Tuition payments are due over the next few years. That means you should add the college years themselves to your time horizon.

The longer your time horizon, the more risk that you can generally take because you have time to ride out a down market. Thus, when you have a long time horizon, most experts would advise that you allocate a good percentage of your portfolio to stocks. If you have a very short time horizon, you may want to consider a CD or a short-term bond.

Second, you must determine your *tolerance for risk*. How much risk can you tolerate, in other words, before you hit the panic button? You probably already have a fairly good idea about your attitude toward risk. Some people, for instance, are *risk averse*. That is, they avoid risk at all costs. These types of investors will only invest in stable investments like T-bills and CDs, even if they have years until they need the money. Other folks will pour all of their money into the stock market and not think twice about it.

Certain factors, however, such as your age, your financial goals, and that old time horizon (that we discussed previously), will affect your willingness, or not, to take risks. Younger people can typically tolerate more risk than older people can, for example, because they have more time to recoup any losses if their investments decrease. However, if you are looking for high growth because you need to build up a significant amount of funds, you will need to accept higher risk levels. Conversely, if you are looking to preserve your existing assets, you should take less risk. Lastly, do not overlook the sleep at night factor. If the risk involved with certain investments causes you to toss and turn at night, you should opt for less risky investments.

Different Types of Risk

When we talk about the risk involved with investing money, there are actually several types of risk. All investments (yes, even savings accounts and T-bills) carry some risk. Stocks are generally considered to be a risky investment, for example, because stock prices can fluctuate so widely, especially over the short term. Unforeseen circumstances, like losing a large client, a fire at company headquarters, or insider fraud, can cause a stock's price to decline. (This type of risk is often called *business* or *company risk*. You can reduce your exposure to this type of risk by investing in a number of different types of stocks rather than the stock of just one or two companies.) The outlook for sales and profits for the company or industry that you are investing in is a good indicator of risk. Are sales expected to grow steadily, for instance? That stock is probably less risky than the stock of a company whose sales come in cyclical fits and starts. Generally speaking, the greater the price volatility of a stock, the greater the risk.

In addition, stock prices move higher and lower depending on the economy, interest rates, and other variables such as the outbreak of war or the passage of a new law. The risk that your particular stock's price will fall simply because the overall stock market has fallen is called *market risk*. You can reduce your exposure to market risk by investing in several different markets such as international and domestic markets and large and small companies.

Bonds often provide steady interest income—and some investors believe, erroneously, that bonds are safe, but bonds carry some risks, too. If interest rates rise, the value of your bond could decline. (Not surprisingly, this is often referred to as *interest rate risk*.) To clarify, let us look at an example. You own a $1,000 bond that pays 6 percent interest. If interest rates rise, and a new investor can buy a $1,000 bond that now pays 7 percent interest could you still sell your 6 percent to another buyer? Probably not without taking a loss. (As stated in Chapter 2, you do not really have to worry about this issue if you plan to hold a bond until maturity.)

Who issued your bond? That is the question you need to ask to determine your credit risk or the risk that a bond's issuer will default on its repayment of the bond. If the U.S. Treasury issues the bond, for example, you have zero risk of losing your principal because bonds issued by the U.S. government are guaranteed. Even though your principal is guaranteed, however, with a T-bill and other safe investments, like savings accounts and CDs, you can still lose money with these investments if your earnings (after taxes) do not keep pace with inflation. This is called *inflation risk*. Let us say that your money market account earns 4 percent per year. Inflation during that period is 3 percent. This means you are really earning just 1 percent. After paying taxes on your interest income, your return on this investment declines even further.

Allocating Your Investments

Investing for your child's college education is like investing for any other long-term goal. Some alternatives are better than others, and diversity is the key to happiness. When should you go for growth, though, and when should you stick with something more secure? The types of investments that you choose will depend (as we discussed previously) on your personality and your willingness to tolerate risk. As an investor, you must always balance the safety and security offered by a conservative investment, like a money market account, with the greater growth potential offered by a riskier investment such as a stock. Again and again, you will come back to this same issue: risk versus return. Which is more important, though? How do you balance these factors?

Timing. It all depends on how much time you have to invest your money. Is your child 5 years away from attending college or 15 years away? When picking an investment for a college fund, your strategy will be influenced by the age of your college-bound child. The general rule is that the closer your child is to attending college, the more conservative your investment should be. Some experts insist, in fact, that the number of years you have before your child attends college is the single most important factor in picking appropriate investments for a college fund.

In the following, we have outlined some strategies for college investments, at various ages: pre-school, elementary, middle school, and high school. These categories make a certain amount of sense, but they are by no means definitive. You may feel that you only need to significantly reallocate assets at three major points in your child's life such as the early years (up to about age eight), the middle years (up to about age 13), and then the older years (up to about age 18). The following allocations, then, are just suggestions to help you get started. Thanks to the guidance (not to mention all that number crunching) of Mari Adam, a certified financial planner and the president of her own financial planning firm, Adam Financial Associates, in Boca Raton, Florida, we have included a conservative approach and a more aggressive approach for each category. Many of you will probably fall somewhere in between. Or perhaps you will pursue a more aggressive approach when your kid is in pre-school, but take a more conservative approach once your kid's in high school. Whether you are working on your own or with a professional financial planner, you will want to design a portfolio to meet your family's exact needs.

Pre-School (Ages 0 to 4)

Now is the time to think *looooong* term. Because you have so much time until your child starts college (and you actually need the money), you can afford to take some risk with your investments, and take advantage of maximum growth. Put a chunk of your money into stocks, and leave it there, even if the market takes a dip. Why? You have time to ride the ups and downs of a market cycle. Over the long term—by that, most experts mean 10 years or so—stocks have consistently delivered the best returns. In the large-cap fund category, Adam suggests that investors split their holdings down the middle. Half of the allocation should be invested in value stocks: typically, that means banks and other financial companies, and food, drug, and energy firms that offer steady, long-term growth. The other half of the allocation should go to growth stocks: technology companies, for instance, that offer greater, faster growth.

If you are taking a more conservative approach, a sample portfolio might include 80 percent equities (spread among large-cap stock funds, growth and income stock funds, aggressive growth stock funds and international stock funds) and 20 percent fixed income (a combination of short-term bonds, intermediate-term bonds and long-term bonds). A more aggressive approach would be entirely in equities.

Elementary (Ages 5 to 9)

You still have plenty of time left to build up a sizable fund. If you are worried about leaving it all invested in stocks, though, it is okay, says Adam, to shift some assets into more moderate risk investments such as intermediate-term corporate bonds. How do you actually make such an investment shift? You can simply call your broker or the mutual fund company itself. In most cases, they will send you some papers to fill out, which will detail which money you want moved (you will have to be specific about the exact fund from which the money is to be moved), where (again, you will have to be specific in terms of the new fund's exact name), when, and how much. Another alternative is to leave the existing funds alone, and simply channel all new money into the new mutual fund(s). Depending on the amount of money you invest each year, you may have to map out the latter strategy well in advance. It could take a couple of years to build up 10 percent, for example, in a new bond fund.

If you are taking a more conservative approach, a sample portfolio might include 70 percent equities (spread among large-cap stock funds, growth and income stock funds, aggressive growth stock funds and international stock funds) and 30 percent fixed income (a combination of short-term and intermediate-term bonds). A more aggressive approach would be 90 percent in equities, with 10 percent allocated to intermediate-term bonds.

Middle School (Ages 10 to 13)

You still have about five to eight years to go, so you do not want to give up on *growth* yet. However, your window of opportunity to take full advantage of investments that offer the highest returns is dwindling. To lower your risk, it is smart to allocate some of your investments to fixed-income funds that protect your capital and provide income, says Adam. This way, you balance your more aggressive growth investments with lower-volatility fixed income investments.

If you are taking a more conservative approach, a sample portfolio might include 50 percent equities (spread among large-cap stock funds, growth and income stock funds, aggressive growth stock funds and international stock funds) and 50 percent in short-term bonds. A more aggressive approach would be 70 percent in equities and 30 percent in intermediate-term bonds.

High School (Ages 14 to 18)

As your child approaches college age, you should start easing some of your money out of stocks and into shorter-term, more conservative investments. Basically, you need to start thinking like a short-term investor, says Adam. With college just three years off, it is too risky (for the average investor) to have all of his or her money invested in stocks. Do not get too conservative, of course. Nix the savings accounts, no matter how risk averse you are. Instead, consider moving some of your money into other higher yielding yet still liquid investments, such as CDs, money market funds, or short-term bonds, that mature when that first college bill arrives. Ideally, you should shift the money needed to pay the first year's worth of college bills into one of these more liquid accounts, and then repeat every year thereafter until your child graduates. This way, you will always have the money ready to pay the upcoming year's tuition, and the remaining money in your portfolio can continue to grow at slightly higher rates.

If you are taking a more conservative approach, a sample portfolio might include 30 percent equities (spread between large-cap stock funds and growth and income stock funds) and 70 percent in short-term bonds. A more aggressive approach would be 60 percent in the same type of equities and 40 percent (allocated between short-term and intermediate-term bonds).

College (Ages 19 to 22)

You do not need to pay for that entire four-year college bill on the first day of freshmen year. You need just one year's worth of payments. (Some colleges will even let you pay in monthly installments.) You have three more years before you need all of your investment money. At this point, though, most people want stability. That is, they do not want go-go growth anymore. They just want their investments to retain their current value. Still, depending on your risk tolerance, this approach could yield various portfolios, says Adam. A very conservative investor may put a hefty chunk of his money in cash investments, such as CDs or money market accounts, for example, that let him write tuition checks directly to the college. A more aggressive investor may shift to mostly fixed-income investments (that mature when annual tuition payments are due) with a small portion still reserved for stocks.

If you are taking a more conservative approach, your sample portfolio may not include *any* equities for this age group, 60 percent in short-term bonds and 40 percent in cash (a combination of CDs and a money market mutual fund that gives you check-writing privileges so you can write checks for tuition and other expenses. If you want a more aggressive approach, consider keeping 10 percent in equities (allocated between large-cap stock funds and growth and income funds), 70 percent in short-term bonds and 20 percent in cash (CDs and a money market mutual fund).

SAFE BETS . . . FOR SHORT-TERM NEEDS

These investments are perfect for money you need to access in the next year or two. You will probably want to plunk some of your funds into a money market account so you can write checks directly from the account to your child's school.

CDs	U.S. T-bills and notes
Money Market mutual funds	Zero coupon bonds (if held to maturity)
U.S. savings bonds	

MODERATE RISK . . . FOR THE NEXT FIVE YEARS

These investments are not quite as safe as those listed previously. The risk is still rather modest, though, which makes these good investments generally for cash you will need in the next five years (or less). In return for this extra risk, you will get a better return on your money.

Growth and income stock mutual funds	Municipal bonds
Balanced funds	Corporate bonds

HIGHER RISK . . . FOR THE LONG TERM

If Junior is still in diapers—and you can tolerate the ups and downs of the stock market—now is the time to invest in these aggressive funds. The potential result: above-average earnings that will get your college fund off to a good start.

Aggressive growth stock mutual funds
Growth stock mutual funds
International and global stock mutual funds
Junk bond mutual funds

Setting Up Your Investments

Once you have decided whether you would like to invest in blue chip stocks, international stocks, or short-term bonds, you will have to work out another important issue: How will you set up your investments? Up until now, we have talked mostly about the investments themselves. That is, stocks, bonds, and mutual funds. Although the issues discussed in picking those investments were important, you now need to make a few more, equally important choices.

Let us assume, for instance, that you want to invest in a mixture of stock and bond mutual funds. You could call your Uncle Stanley on the phone (or your broker, if you have one) and tell him just that: "I have been thinking and I have decided that I want to invest in these mutual funds for my daughter's college education." Great idea, he will say. Were you planning on investing those in your name, or hers? "Hmm. What is the difference?" you ask. Good question. *That is issue number one:* Do you want to set up a custodial account for your child, or do you want to simply invest the money in your name? You will find the information that can help you answer these questions in the "Investing in Your Name or Theirs?" section.

Should you decide that you would like to invest the money in your daughter's name, you will then have another issue to contend with, and this is issue number two: Do you want to set up a regular taxable account, or a Coverdell education savings account? Coverdell education savings accounts grow tax free, for example, but they have an annual contribution limit. Taxable custodial accounts have no such limits, but they can severely hurt your chances of getting financial aid because you can save an unlimited amount of money. There is more complete information about Coverdell education savings accounts later in this chapter.

Finally, would you like to simply leave the driving (investment-wise) to somebody else? Investing in a mixture of stocks and bonds for little Charlie certainly sounds like a good idea. Sign me up, you say. However, making sure that you move some of those stocks to bonds when she is around 12 and then—what was it again?—selling some of those bonds and buying CDs when she is 18? This is issue number three: If this investment stuff sounds too overwhelming, you could leave the asset management to others (or at least get someone to help you). Hire a recommended, qualified, all around practically perfect financial advisor for professional guidance. (Chapter 5 explains what these financial pros can do, and how to pick one.) You could always ask Uncle Stanley for help, of course, but, personally, I have never found relatives to give good financial advice (unless they are trained professionals and even then it is questionable). The other alternative is to sign up for a state-sponsored college savings plan that manages the investments for you. This option is so hot these days that an entire chapter is dedicated to these *529 plans*—as they are often called because of the tax code that governs them—and their older brothers, the Prepaid Tuition Plans (see Chapter 4 for the scoop).

Investing in Your Name or Theirs?

Should the money be invested in your name or your child's name? The answer, generally, is not as straightforward as it might appear. The tax law can make it attractive, for example, to invest the money in your child's name. However, in doing so, you give up control of the money, and you may adversely affect your chances of getting financial aid. Before making this decision, then, you must consider the tax implications, the control issue, and the effect on financial aid. Each issue will be discussed in detail in the following.

Understanding the Tax Implications

Whether you invest in CDs, stocks, or bonds, the money that you invest will hopefully earn more money. It is called interest or income, depending on the type of investment, and you must pay tax on those earnings just as you pay tax on your weekly paycheck. That much we all know, right?

In most cases, children are in a lower tax bracket than adults.

That means they will pay less in taxes on those investment earnings than you would because, as an adult, you are probably taxed at a higher rate. Therefore, you could save money in taxes by putting that college fund in your daughter's name. (The money, after all, is being saved to pay for *her* college education.)

That is the theory anyway. Unfortunately, it does not work quite that smoothly anymore. In 1987, the tax laws changed, making it less advantageous (for some families) to save money in a child's name, especially for a child who is under the age of 14.

Here is how the tax laws work now: Since 1987, children must pay taxes on the interest earned on investments. (This is called unearned income because you do not actually work for this money.) How much your child must pay in taxes depends on her age and the amount she earned through those investments. The first $750 in unearned income in 2003, for example, is completely tax-free. The second $750 is taxed at 10 percent, the lowest bracket for federal income tax. Up until this point, then, it pays, from a tax standpoint, to save money in the child's name. It is costing you less in taxes.

Once your child's accounts start earning more than $1,500 (that is $750 + $750) per year, however, it starts to get tricky, and in some cases, less of a tax-saver. If your child is under age 14, for example, any unearned income above that first $1,500 is taxed at the rate that you (the child's parents) pay on their own income. Known as the *Kiddie Tax*, this arrangement is meant to discourage parents from sheltering money in their child's name. When kids turn 14, however, they pay a child's tax rate (again, usually 15 percent) on any unearned income above $1,500.

Now, why is this tax savings so important? Whenever you can avoid paying taxes on investments, you are actually speeding up the growth of that money because you are not only keeping money that would have otherwise gone to the government, but you are also earning interest on that money. That is the tax story. Now let us look at the issue of control.

Whom Do You Want in Control of the Money?

When you put money in a child's name, you are basically giving up control of that money. At age 18 (or 21, in some states), your child may decide to use the money for college as you planned, or he may decide to take an extended vacation in Europe instead.

Minors cannot control money, even when you set up a custodial account for them such as a Uniform Gifts to Minors Act (UGMA) or a Uniform Transfers to Minors Act (UTMA). In most cases, the parent will act as the account's custodian and as such, have full control over the use of the money in the account. That is the good news. However, money or assets that are put into a UGMA or UTMA account are *irrevocable*. That is, you cannot get the money back once it has been given. However, did I not just say that you have full control over the money while your child is a minor? You have control over how the money is spent as long as the money is used to pay for your child's expenses (and not yours). The money does not necessarily have to be used for college. You could, for example, use the money in a custodial account to pay for summer camp, karate lessons, or a piano for your budding Chopin. You cannot, however, use the money to buy a summer home or take a family vacation. Well, at least you are not supposed to. No one is actually watching to make sure that you use the funds for little Harry only. In fact, the only person who would file a complaint and possibly take you to court over misuse of the funds is little Harry himself. Having said that, I am not advocating, of course, that you set up a UGMA and plan to pay the mortgage with it. Rather, do not be frightened by the word irrevocable. It is not quite as final as it sounds. The money does not necessarily have to be used for college, and there are a lot of other ways you can spend the money on your child.

Once your child reaches maturity, however, it is a different story. In most states, the age of majority is 18. (In other states, it is 21.) At that time—listen: Do you hear the boom being lowered now?—the money in a custodial account becomes the property of the child. That is right, the money belongs to little Harry, and he can do whatever he wants with it, even if it is not the intended purpose of the funds such as paying for a college education. Despite what you may think about your child now and how he would never simply blow the money, children have been known to spend the money in these accounts on things other than college. What if, for instance, your child simply does not go to college? Or he would prefer to take a few years off first finding himself in the south of France? By law, you (the parent) no longer have control over the money. You cannot tell him he must use the money for college or else. (You can tell him, of course, but he does not have to listen!)

If the age of maturity is 21 in your state, this may be less of an issue to you. Your child will have already attended two or three years of college, and thus spent a good portion of the fund on her tuition by age 21. That is assuming, of course, that she goes to college. If your daughter decides that a higher education is not for her, she cannot touch the money, in this case, until she is 21. At that time, the money is still hers—that means she could spend it all, at that point, on a red Ferrari convertible. That is the control situation. Now let us look at how money invested in a child's name affects financial aid.

A CHILD'S SAVINGS CAN MEAN LESS FINANCIAL AID

Colleges think that a student should spend her own money, rather than yours, on college. As assets increase (and income, too, but we will deal with that later in the book), financial aid decreases. We will be talking more about financial aid in subsequent chapters. The point that you need to understand here: When it comes to calculating the amount of aid that a student will receive, the student is expected to kick in a larger share of his or her own assets (35 percent, in fact) than you, the parent, are expected to contribute of your assets (just 5.6 percent). In short, money invested in a child's name counts more, according to colleges, toward footing the tuition bill than money held in a parent's name. As a result, the student might qualify for less financial aid than if the money had been in his parent's name. So, if you think that your family will qualify for financial aid, keep the funds in your name.

Let us look at an example. From his earnings at part-time jobs, several summers spent mowing lawns, and various monetary gifts received from your relatives over the years, your college-age son Daniel has managed to save $20,000. The money is in a mutual fund in his name. When young Daniel applies for financial aid, the powers that be (in this case, the financial aid officers) will tell him that $7,000 of that fund (that is 35 percent of $20,000) can be used to pay his tuition. Next year, and the year after that (until he graduates), they will tell him the same thing: You must use 35 percent of the remaining balance to pay for your education.

Now, let us imagine that you have that same $20,000 saved. However, it was saved in your name instead. This time, when the financial aid officers look at the application, they use a different formula. Because it is not the student's money—but yours, the parent's—the schools figure not quite as much should be expected to be used for school. Instead of kicking in $7,000, you will have to shell out $1,120 (or, 5.6 percent of $20,000) that first year. Again, we will talk more about financial aid in Chapter 7, but federal aid formulas do not consider retirement savings accounts or the equity in your home as an asset. For many middle class people, that is where the lion's share of their savings is stashed: 401(k)s and their home. In addition, not every cent of a parent's assessable assets must count toward paying for college, says Brian E. Glickman, a certified public accountant who runs Tuition Solutions, a college financial planning firm in Smithtown, New York. The FAFSA has an *asset protection allowance*, based on a parent's age and marital status, which keeps a minimum amount of parental assets out of the financial aid formula. If one partner of a married couple is age 50, for example, $48,400 of that couple's assets would not be included in the financial aid calculation. (See Table 3.1).

If you discover that you will be eligible for financial aid but that the amount will be decreased because of the money saved in your son's name, do not give up just yet. You may be able to wiggle around the issue and qualify for that aid.

TABLE 3.1   Asset Protection Allowance

AGE OF STUDENT OR AGE OF OLDER PARENT	MARRIED OR TWO PARENTS	SINGLE OR ONE PARENT
25	$0	$0
26	$2,500	$1,600
27	$5,000	$3,200
28	$7,500	$4,800
29	$10,000	$6,400
30	$12,500	$8,000
31	$15,000	$9,600
32	$17,500	$11,200
33	$19,900	$12,900
34	$22,400	$14,500
35	$24,900	$16,100
36	$27,400	$17,700
37	$29,900	$19,300
38	$32,400	$20,900
39	$34,900	$22,500
40	$37,400	$24,100
41	$38,400	$24,500
42	$39,400	$25,100
43	$40,400	$25,600
44	$41,400	$26,200
45	$42,500	$26,800
46	$43,500	$27,400
47	$44,600	$28,000
48	$45,800	$28,700
49	$46,900	$29,400
50	$48,400	$30,100
51	$49,600	$30,700
52	$50,900	$31,600

AGE OF STUDENT OR AGE OF OLDER PARENT	MARRIED OR TWO PARENTS	SINGLE OR ONE PARENT
53	$52,500	$32,300
54	$53,800	$33,100
55	$55,400	$33,900
56	$57,100	$34,700
57	$58,900	$35,700
58	$60,700	$36,500
59	$62,500	$37,600
60	$64,400	$38,700
61	$66,600	$39,700
62	$69,000	$40,900
63	$71,000	$42,000
64	$73,400	$43,200
65+	$75,900	$44,400

Here is how: Use the money in the custodial account to pay for everything for your child that you would otherwise use your own funds for. Throw him a graduation party; buy him a car or a new laptop to take with him to school; send him on that grand tour of Europe. Then, use as much of the funds as you can to pay for that first and (if necessary) second year of college. Once the custodial account is depleted, you can then apply for financial aid (which is recalculated every year) for the remaining years of college.

MAKING A DECISION WHEN YOU ARE ON THE FENCE FINANCIALLY

We have looked at the advantages and disadvantages of investing college funds in your child's name. From a financial standpoint, you must now decide what is more valuable: the tax savings or the possible future financial aid. Again, this decision is trickier than it appears at first. You have to make a decision *now*— years in advance of when you will actually know if you qualify for aid or not. How do you decide, then? Toss a coin. (Just kidding.) If your income is high and you can already clearly foresee that you will not qualify for aid, the tax break makes the most sense. (Chapter 7 offers an explanation of financial aid qualifications that should help.) In general, though, if your annual income is over $125,000 and you only have one child in college at a time, you probably will not qualify for aid. That is a ballpark estimate. Conversely, if your income is low and you can already foresee that you will probably qualify for aid, keep the money in your name and hope for the best. Of course, you may be in the middle, which is where many parents find themselves. At this point in time, you may be sitting on that proverbial fence. You may qualify for aid. Then again, you may not. Not surprisingly, this middle ground is often the trickiest water to tread.

In almost every case, financial aid advantages dwarf tax advantages when using custodial accounts—regardless of your tax bracket, says Raymond D. Loewe, a chartered financial consultant and the president of College Money, a college financial planning firm in Marlton, New Jersey. Still, if you really cannot decide whether you should go with the financial aid and the tax savings, then the deciding factor, suggests Loewe, should be *control*. Do you want your kid to have control of the money? Can you trust that he or she will use the money for college as you intended? If you are not sure, leave the money in your name until the child turns 14, says Loewe. Taxes are not as big an issue before that time. At age 14, look at your income and find out if you are likely to qualify for financial aid. If you are, then keep the money in your name. If you are not likely to qualify for aid, and you strongly believe that your child is headed for college and that she will be responsible enough to handle the money at age 18, then consider putting the money in your child's name at that point to reap those tax advantages.

Still not convinced? Here is another thought. Investing in your own name makes even more sense if you have more than one child. Why? I have three young children, all of whom at this point are headed for college, and there is not a scholar or a football star among the lot, yet. It is a leveled playing field, so to speak. In 10 years, who knows? My middle son may get a scholarship. Then what happens to the money saved in his name? He spends it on an extended vacation when I could easily use that money to pay for a better school for my other two children, or even to bolster my own retirement savings. Philip C. Johnson, a financial planner in Clifton Park, New York, who specializes in college planning, proposes a similar theory. In most cases, families would do well to just invest for the long term, he says, and keep the money in their (that is the parents') name. Such an arrangement gives you the option of using the funds, in the future, to best suit your needs. That could be a vacation home in Bimini, a red convertible for you to tool around town in when you have retired, or, yes, college tuition for your kids.

Coverdell Education Savings Accounts (ESAs)

If you want to save money for college in the student's name but retain control over investments and disbursements, you can use a Coverdell Education Savings Account (ESA), formerly called an education IRA. You set the account up through a bank, brokerage firm or mutual fund.

You can contribute up to $2,000 each year for each child under age 18. The child need not be *your* child—you can contribute for your niece, grandchild or a friend's child. But you are only eligible to make contributions if your adjusted gross income (AGI) is not more than $95,000 (or $190,000 on a joint return). The contribution limit phases out for AGI over this amount and is completely phased out so that no contributions can be made if AGI is more than $110,000 ($220,000 on a joint return).

Like IRAs, contributions to Coverdell ESAs can be made up to the due date of your return for the year (e.g., 2002 contributions can be made up to April 15, 2003). Contributions can be made to *both* these accounts as well as to qualified tuition plans (discussed in Chapter 4).

Funds from Coverdell ESAs can be used tax free not only for higher education purposes, but also to pay school expenses for grades K through 12, at both public and private schools. Of course, if money is withdrawn for high school, it will not be there to pay for college. Qualified expenses include computers, Internet access, tutoring, after-school activities and more. But if funds are withdrawn for nonqualified purposes, a 10% penalty applies in addition to income tax on the earnings.

Funds must be used before the beneficiary reaches age 30 (unless he or she is a special-needs child who requires more time to complete an education). At that time, earnings on funds remaining in the account become taxed to the beneficiary. But this tax can be avoided by transferring the account to another beneficiary who is related (including a sibling, first cousin, child or grandchild).

Funds can be withdrawn from a Coverdell ESA tax free in the same year that an education credit is claimed (as explained in Chapter 6). But there's no double dipping—the distribution cannot be used to pay the same expenses for which the credit is claimed.

CHAPTER 4

Tuition Savings Plans

What is the hottest trend in college savings? 529 plans. Called *529s* because of the section of the U.S. tax code that governs them, these handy little tools have evolved over the last decade from your basic prepaid tuition plan (with its lackluster earnings and in-state school restrictions) to a tax-saving, tax-deductible, go-to-any-school-in-the-country, tuition-saving machine.

All states now have a savings plan (Washington's plan begins in mid-2003), and many are adding options, easing their restrictions, and/or hiring a professional money-management firm, such as Fidelity Investments or TIAA-CREF, to revamp their plans and, thus, draw more investors. Earnings from these investment accounts are now *tax-free* for federal income tax purposes—instead of just tax-deferred as in the past—if the money is used to pay for certain higher education expenses.

So, just how good are these plans, really? Should they be part of your college savings plan? Some financial experts have been cited in the business press, praising these plans as one of the best savings vehicles for college. To a large extent, that is true. There are numerous advantages (which will be discussed in detail in the next section) and, frankly, there is not a whole lot of competition out there. The Coverdell Education Savings Account, or ESA), for example, does not let you save enough. Yes, the annual investment amount is now $2,000, and yes, the income restrictions have been raised to more reasonable levels. However, some families are still locked out and a $2,000 annual investment just will not do the job for many families, especially those who are beginning to save rather late in the game. Custodial accounts do not save you that much in taxes when all is said and done. To get those savings, you have to give the control of the money to the kids. What is left? Taxable accounts, which force you to give a sizable chunk of your profits to Uncle Sam. (See Table 4.1).

That does not mean, of course, that 529 plans will work for every family. However, 529s offer so many advantages that it seems that you cannot devise a winning college strategy without at least investigating these plans.

A New Twist on an Old Theme

If it seems like you have heard about these types of plans a long time ago and did not give them a second thought because they were those state school things, you are right. College savings plans are not exactly new. In the late 1980s, states began offering 529s. However, these earlier versions were all *prepaid* plans. That is, you paid a set amount—in advance—for college. Some parents liked this arrangement because it protected them against the rising cost of tuition. (This was especially true when the plans first appeared on the scene because the rate of college inflation was higher than it is today.) No matter how high tuition prices rose, these parents had locked-in the future cost of tuition at current prices. Prepaid plans are still offered by many states, and for some folks, they are the perfect college investment plan, especially in view of the stock market's performance in the past several years. (The details of these plans will be discussed in the Prepaid section later in this chapter.) The drawback of prepaid plans is (and always has been) that the money is really meant to pay for an in-state public university. If your kid does not want to attend State U., you have to make up the difference. Yes, most plans now let you use the funds to pay for tuition at private schools or out-of-state schools not covered under the plan, but the amount you may need to meet the tuition at those other schools, in addition to the money plunked into a prepaid plan, can be considerable.

Fortunately, the prepaid plans are just one side of the 529 coin. Turn this tired old nickel over and you will find the *new* 529s. These are not prepaid plans, but *savings* plans in which you can set aside money in a variety of investments. Depending on the state that offers the 529 plan, those investments can range from conservative money market funds to aggressive growth stock funds. Thus, your investment returns will be market driven—much like the funds that your IRA or 401(k) plan is invested in—so you have the potential to earn more money. (Remember, the money invested in a prepaid plan is based solely on tuition inflation.) Of course, if a 529 savings plan is invested solely in stocks, you could *lose* money, something that's happened to many in the past several years.

This opportunity to invest in stocks and bonds is one reason that everyone is talking about 529s these days. A big attraction of these plans, though, is the potential tax savings. The money stashed in a 529 grows federal (and often state) tax-free. In addition, residents of some states have the opportunity to save even more. Some 529s let residents deduct all or a portion of their contributions to their 529 plan. (What each state offers is outlined in the discussion of the particular plans later in this chapter.)

TABLE 4.1 How Do 529 Plans Stack Up?

	PREPAID PLANS	529 SAVINGS PLANS	COVERDELL ESAS	TAXABLE MUTUAL FUND IN THE PARENT'S NAME	UGMA/ UTMA
How Much Can You Invest?	Varies by state, typically $15,000 to $30,000	Varies by state, typically $100,000 to $250,000	$2,000 per year (under the new tax year), per child, up to age 18	Unlimited	Unlimited
Who Controls the Account?	The account owner (not the beneficiary)	The account owner (not the beneficiary)	The account owner (not the beneficiary)	The parent	The child, at age of majority
Tax Treatment	Tax-free withdrawals (under the new tax law)	Tax-free withdrawals (under the new tax law) Income tax deductions available in many states; exemptions on state taxes in many states.	Earnings are tax-free if used for qualified education expenses.	No federal or state tax benefits	A limited amount may be federal tax exempt; at least a portion of the earnings are taxable at student's lower rate.
Restrictions on Use of Money	Withdrawals must be used for qualified higher education expenses; often limited to in-state schools.	Withdrawals must be used for qualified higher education expenses; can be used at schools nationwide.	Withdrawals must be used for qualified education expenses; generally must use money by age 30.	None	Must be used for the benefit of the student

(continued)

TABLE 4.1 How Do 529 Plans Stack Up? *(continued)*

	PREPAID PLANS	529 SAVINGS PLANS	COVERDELL ESAS	TAXABLE MUTUAL FUND IN THE PARENT'S NAME	UGMA/ UTMA
Financial Aid Considerations	Withdrawals reduce financial aid dollar for dollar under the federal aid formula.	Earnings are counted as income to the student. Will reduce federal aid 50 cents on every dollar, above a certain minimum level.	Counted as the student's asset; 35% of student's assets figure into financial aid calculation.	Counted as the parent's asset; 5.6% of parent's assets figure into financial aid calculation.	Counted as the student's asset; 35% of student's assets figure into financial aid calculation.
Advantages	Contributions may be made by anyone; no family income restrictions.	Contributions may be made by anyone; no family income restrictions, account owner retains control of assets; plans can be transferred to another family member without penalty.	Can transfer account to another child; contributions may be made by anyone; assets may be used to pay elementary and secondary school expenses.	Wide variety of investment choices; no income restrictions; parents retain control of the assets; the money does not have to be used for college.	Contributions may be made by anyone; no family income restrictions.
Disadvantages	Some states will not permit funds to be used for out-of-state schools; typically offer, fixed, low rate of return; 10% penalty for non-qualified withdrawals.	10% penalty on earnings for non-qualified withdrawals; account owners may only change investment options once per year or when the beneficiary is changed.	Penalty for non-qualified withdrawals; income restrictions; relatively low contribution limit.	The parent is taxed annually at the capital gains rate.	No tax-advantaged growth; student gains complete control of money at age of majority; contributions are not deductible.

Source: Strong Capital Management, Inc. Reprinted with permission.

All withdrawals made from a 529 plan on January 1, 2002 and later are federal tax-free. That change alone may convince many parents to invest in a 529. However—and there is always some catch with these things—this federal tax exemption will expire in 2011 unless congress makes it permanent. If you are saving for a three-year old now, will you still be able to take the money out of your 529 plan tax free in 15 years when you need it? Of course, if your child is currently 10 years of age or older, then you do not have to worry about the tax advantage disappearing before you get to use it.

Taxes are not the 529's only attractive feature:

- *There is no income limit for contributors.* It does not matter if you earn $50,000 or $500,000. Everyone can invest in a 529 plan. A Coverdell ESA does have an income cap. (See Chapter 6.)
- *You, the investor, retain control of the funds.* Unlike traditional custodial accounts, which become the property of the child at age 18 or 21, a 529 plan remains under your control.
- *More investment choices.* Some of the earlier 529 savings plans turned investors off because those plans offered such limited investment choices. Now, 529 savings plans offer a plethora of choices ranging from technology stock funds and short-term bond funds to age-based portfolios that automatically change asset allocations over time, based on the age of your child. Typically, these plans move from more aggressive to less aggressive investments as the student approaches college age. One plan, for instance, invests 88 percent of the portfolio in stocks and the remaining 12 percent in bonds until the child is age three. By the time that same child is between 15 and 17 years old, the portfolio would have shifted to 37 percent in stocks, 20 percent in money market funds, and 43 percent in bonds.
- *More school choices.* Unlike the prepaid 529 plans that are set up to help you pay for in-state public colleges, the money invested in a 529 savings plan can be used at any public or private college or graduate school in the country. In this case, however, a Coverdell ESA is even more flexible. It can be used to pay for private elementary and high schools, too.
- *You can transfer the account to another member of the family without penalty.* If your child does not go to college, for example, or if she gets a scholarship, you can transfer the account to another child or another family member (e.g., brother, sister, stepchild, first cousins).

The Drawbacks of 529 Savings Plans

Like most other investments, the 529 is not a complete win-win situation. You must give up certain features to secure the tax savings and other perks. One major drawback, for example, is your loss of investment control. Although most states now let you design (to some degree) your own investment portfolio—your choices can range from all stocks to all bonds to some combination of stocks and fixed income—once you select a savings portfolio, that is it. You cannot change your investment selection whenever you want to. Once you have chosen an investment mix for your contributions, the money that you have invested (and the earnings on that money) generally must stay invested in that initial allocation until the money is withdrawn (you can make changes once a year or when you change beneficiaries).

How then can you swing some old asset allocation to reduce your investment risk? You can put any future contributions into a different investment mix.

What if you want to reallocate your existing 529 assets? You may not be able to move the money invested in stocks into another investment *within that particular state plan*. However, you can move the money you have invested in that state plan to a completely different state plan. Let us assume again that you have been investing in stocks within New York State's plan. Now, however, you want a mixture of stocks and bonds, so you take the money out of the New York plan and reinvest it in, say, Utah's plan. You can move from one state plan to another with relative ease. How frequently can you switch? You can change once in a 12-month period, but you must make the switch within 60 days.

A third option is to let the 529 handle asset allocation for you. The 529's age-based portfolios gradually shift your investments from more aggressive investments to more conservative ones, as your child ages. Obviously, this method will involve the least amount of work because the plan makes these changes for you. The trouble is, however, that most of these age-based portfolios show "a definite conservative approach," Says Raymond D. Loewe, a chartered financial consultant and the president of College Money, a college financial planning firm in Marlton, New Jersey. The state plans may think they are just being prudent, he says, but an increase in college inflation (which is higher than general inflation now, but not as high as it had been in recent years) could eat into these conservative portfolios very quickly. Still, if you are overwhelmed by the process of asset allocation, this might be the best route for you because the job is managed by the money management firm that manages the 529 plan.

Financial aid, of course, is another important factor. At first glance, it can seem like the money will not impact a student's chances of getting financial aid as severely as other savings. Why? The money in a 529 plan is treated as an asset of the custodian, and generally, that is the parents. (The student is the beneficiary.) Some folks will have you believe that because those assets are not the student's, such savings will not impact the child's financial aid. However, that is simply misleading, and, in some ways, just not true. First, when people talk about 529s not affecting financial aid, they are talking about *state* aid, says Loewe, not federal aid. "State financial aid is not always a very large portion of a financial aid package," says Loewe. "Some states offer aid only to residents who attend schools within their own state."

What is more, the earnings from your 529 investments may not count as a student's assets, but they do count as *income* to the student. Students are expected to contribute more of their income to pay their tuition—federal guidelines demand 50 percent of a student's income (above a certain level)—than their parents are expected to contribute from their own incomes. The only way, in fact, that the asset does not figure into the financial aid calculation, says Loewe, is if the custodian is not the parent of the student. (Perhaps a grandparent or an aunt or uncle has opened an account for your child.)

Prepaid Plans

Michigan, Florida, and Wyoming created the first prepaid tuition programs 15 years ago. Today, some 19 states offer these original 529 plans, which let you lock into tomorrow's college costs at today's prices. Conservative investors might like these prepaid plans because basically you are buying a sure thing. Parents contribute money to the plan while their child is young. In return, the state guarantees to cover all or a portion of the tuition costs (depending on how much you contribute) when their kid enters a state college or university years later. Other investments, obviously, cannot offer such a guarantee. However, most other investments, such as a stock funds within the 529 *savings* plans, would probably earn a much better yield than any of these plans over time.

Still, what happens if Junior wins a scholarship or decides he does not want to go to Alabama State after all? If your child wins a scholarship, you may still be able to use the money invested in a prepaid plan to pay for tuition. Scholarship money is generally more flexible and may be used to cover other expenses such as dormitory, meal plan, or book costs. If your child does not want to go to the state schools, most plans now enable you to transfer the funds to an out-of-state public college or even a private university. (Some states do not, though, so be sure to check this out before investing.) You will probably have to fork over some more dough. Public colleges may charge you higher nonresident rates, and private schools, well, they just cost more than a state school. If your son decides to skip college altogether, you generally can get back what you contributed. With interest? That varies from one state plan to the next. (Again, check out this little feature in advance.) You will be hit with a federal penalty—it is 10 percent

---

FYI

To find out about the 529 plan(s) available in your state, call the National Association of State Treasurers at 877-277-6496. Two helpful web sites are *www.collegesavings.org* and *www.savingforcollege.com*.

of earnings—for any money withdrawn that is not used for higher education. That rule does not vary by state; it is a federal requirement.

Most plans let you invest annually or monthly. Other features, such as payroll deduction and automatic transfer from a checking or savings account, make it easy to set aside money regularly. In most cases, you and/or the student must be a resident of the state to sign up with that particular plan. Also, you must sign up for these plans during a specific enrollment period. In Maryland, for instance, enrollment is permitted from October through February. All enrollment forms received after a state's deadline will be returned and are subject to next year's contract price increases. Newborns, however, may be enrolled at any time.

How much will you pay? The cost to prepay tuition at your state's public schools is calculated using three variables:

1. *The number of years of college tuition that you purchase.* In the following list of examples, I am using costs for a four-year university.

2. *The age of your child.* The price for a toddler is less than the price for a teenager.

3. *The payment plan selected.* Lump sum payments cost less than monthly payments extended over many years.

In addition, you will pay an assortment of fees, which vary from state to state. Some states charge one-time application fees of $75 or more; other schools charge $15 or $20 if you want to change the beneficiary on the account; other states charge $15 or $25 to transfer your funds to an out-of-state school. (One school actually charges $25 *per semester* to do this.) Still others charge an additional $20 or $25 to change your projected college enrollment date.

ALABAMA

Prepaid Affordable College Tuition (PACT)

800-252-7228

www.treasury.state.al.us

Enrollment period: September.

Cost: In 2002, it cost $11,413 in one lump sum (or $105 per month, for 223 months) to prepay four years of tuition and fees for a newborn.

Payment options: A single, lump-sum payment, a five-year plan of 60 monthly payments, an extended plan of monthly payments until the child reaches college age.

State tax advantages: Earnings are exempt from state income tax if the money is used (as planned) for college.

Guarantee: No.

Applicable in-state, public schools: 15 universities, 35 community colleges, 2 junior colleges, 7 technical colleges, and 1 senior college.

COLORADO

CollegeInvest

Prepaid Tuition Fund

800-478-5651

www.collegeinvest.org

The fund is closed to new enrollments while it is being restructured.

FLORIDA

Florida Prepaid College Program

800-552-4723

www.florida529plans.com

Enrollment period: November through January.

Cost: In 2002, it cost a lump sum of $8,240.90 (or $62.88 per month, for 223 months) to prepay four years of tuition and fees for a newborn.

Payment options: A single lump-sum payment, monthly payments extended until your child reaches college age, a five-year plan of 60 monthly payments.

State tax advantages: None (Florida does not have an income tax).

Guarantee: The plan is guaranteed by the state of Florida.

Applicable in-state, public schools: 11 universities and 28 community colleges, as well as in-state private colleges and most out-of-state colleges.

ILLINOIS

College Illinois!

877-877-3724

www.collegeillinois.com

Enrollment period: October through March (newborns to August).

Cost: In 2001, it will cost a lump sum of $16,892 (or $207 per month, for 10 years) to prepay four years of tuition and fees for a newborn.

Payment options: Annual payments for 5 or 10 years. (You can also make a down payment and then make reduced annual payments for 5 or 10 years.)

State tax advantages: None.

Guarantee: The plan is guaranteed by the state of Illinois.

Applicable in-state, public schools: Not available.

KENTUCKY

Kentucky's Affordable Prepaid Tuition Plan (KAPT)

888-919-KAPT

www.getKAPT.com

Enrollment period: September 22, 2003, through January 26, 2004 (newborns accepted year-round).

Cost: In 2002, it will cost a lump-sum payment of $16,338 (or 204 monthly payments of $134) to prepay tuition and fees for a newborn at a four-year public university.

Payment options: A single lump-sum payment, monthly installments, and monthly installments with a down payment.

State tax advantages: Earnings are exempt from state income tax if the money is used (as planned) for college.

Guarantee: None.

Applicable in-state, public schools: 34 four-year public and private universities and 36 community and technical colleges.

MARYLAND

Maryland Prepaid College Trust

888-4MD-GRAD

www.collegeswingsmd.org.

Enrollment period: Ends March 14, 2003

Cost: In 2002, it cost a lump sum of $25,022 (or $216 per month for 204 months) to prepay four years of tuition and fees for a newborn.

Payment options: Lump sum, annual payments, monthly payments for five years, extended monthly payments until the child reaches college age.

State tax advantages: You can deduct up to $2,500 of the contributions made each year on your Maryland state income tax, for each contract that you have purchased. Payments in excess of $2,500 per contract can be deducted from your Maryland state income tax in future years, until the full amount of your payments have been deducted. Earnings are exempt from state income tax if the money is used (as planned) for college.

Guarantee: The plan is backed by a legislative guarantee.

Applicable in-state, public schools: 13 universities and 18 community colleges.

MASSACHUSETTS

The U Plan Prepaid Tuition Program

800-449-6332

www.mefa.org/uplan

Enrollment period: May 1 to June 15.

Cost: Rates vary, depending if you want to prepay a public or a private school. In 2002, it will cost a lump sum of $5,212 to prepay fees and tuition at the University of Massachusetts, Amherst four-year public college, for a newborn. A private school like Wellesley would cost $25,504.

Payment options: A single lump-sum payment or yearly payments. There is not a monthly payment option.

State tax advantages: Earnings are exempt from state income tax if the money is used (as planned) for college.

Guarantee: The plan is backed by a special form of a Massachusetts general obligation bond.

Applicable in-state, public schools: 83 participating schools, which include four-year public and private colleges and community colleges.

MICHIGAN

Michigan Education Trust (MET)

800-638-4543

www.michigan.gov/treasury

Enrollment period: Ends August 31.

Cost: In 2002, it cost $24,252 in one lump sum (or $296 per month, for 120 months) to prepay four years of tuition and fees for a newborn.

Payment options: Lump-sum payment or monthly payments.

State tax advantages: Contributions can be deducted from state income tax.

Guarantee: None.

Applicable in-state, public schools: 15 universities and 28 community colleges.

MISSISSIPPI

Mississippi Prepaid Affordable College Tuition Program (MPACT)

800-987-4450

www.treasury.state.ms.us

Enrollment period: September 1–November 30.

Cost: In 2002, it cost a lump sum of $12,067 (or $105 per month for 208 months) to prepay four years of tuition and fees for a newborn.

Payment options: Lump sum payment, monthly payments, a combination of the two.

State tax advantages: Earnings are exempt from state income tax if the money is used (as planned) for college. Contributions are deductible on your state income tax.

Guarantee: The plan is backed by the full faith and credit of the state of Mississippi.

Applicable in-state, public schools: 8 four-year universities, 14 community colleges, and one junior college.

NEVADA

Nevada Prepaid Tuition

888-477-2667

Enrollment period: To be announced.

Cost: In 2001, it will cost a lump sum of $7,460 (or $149 for 60 months) to prepay four years of tuition and fees for a newborn. The plan was closed in 2002 and will reopen in February 2003.

Payment options: One lump-sum payment, equal monthly payments until the child reaches college age, a five-year option of 60 equal payments, a down payment of at least $1,000 can reduce your monthly payments.

State tax advantages: None.

Guarantee: None.

Applicable in-state, public schools: Not available.

NEW MEXICO

The Education Plan's Prepaid Tuition Program

800-499-7581

www.tepnm.com

Enrollment period: September 1 to December 31.

Cost: In 2002, it will cost a lump-sum payment of $9,984 to prepay four years of tuition and fees for a newborn at a comprehensive university. A research university will cost $14,296.

Payment options: Prepay the full contract amount in one lump sum, make equal monthly or quarterly payments until your child enters college, or devise your own payment plan.

State tax advantages: Earnings are exempt from state income tax if the money is used (as planned) for college. Contributions are deductible on your state income tax.

Guarantee: None.

Applicable in-state, public schools: 10 universities, 6 colleges and 3 community colleges.

OHIO

CollegeAdvantage Guaranteed Savings Fund

800-233-6734

www.collegeadvantage.com

Enrollment period: No enrollment period.

Cost: In 2003, it will cost a lump sum of $30,200 (or $148 paid in 216 monthly payments) to prepay four years of tuition and fees for a newborn.

Payment options: A single lump-sum payment or monthly payments.

State tax advantages: Contributions are deductible on your state income tax. Earnings are exempt from state income tax if the money is used (as planned) for college.

Guarantee: The plan is backed by the full faith and credit of the state of Ohio.

Applicable in-state, public schools: 13 four-year colleges and a number of community and technical colleges.

PENNSYLVANIA

Tap 529 Guaranteed Savings Plan

800-440-4000

www.patap.org

Enrollment period: Open year-round.

Cost: In 2003, it will cost a lump-sum payment of $32,475 to prepay four years of tuition and fees for a newborn at an in-state, public school. An Ivy League school will cost $106,992 (rates change in September 2003).

Payment options: Prepay the full contract amount in one lump sum, make equal monthly or quarterly payments until your child enters college, or devise your own payment plan.

State tax advantages: Earnings are exempt from Pennsylvania state and local income tax if the money is used (as planned) for college.

Guarantee: None.

Applicable in-state, public schools: 4 state-related universities, 14 state universities, and 15 community colleges.

SOUTH CAROLINA

South Carolina Tuition Prepayment Program (SCTPP)

888-772-4723

www.SCgrad.org

Enrollment period: October 1 to January 31 (newborns year-round).

Cost: In 2002, it cost a lump sum of $19,267 (or $161 per month for 221 months) to prepay four years of tuition and fees for a newborn.

Payment options: A single lump-sum payment, 48 monthly payments, and monthly payments extended over the number of years until your child enters college. You can also make a down payment in any amount to lower your monthly payments or to shorten your contract term.

State tax advantages: There is an unlimited deduction for contributions. Earnings are exempt from state income tax if the money is used (as planned) for college.

Guarantee: In the event that the program should ever be discontinued, the state guarantees that your contributions, plus 4% interest, will be refunded.

Applicable in-state, public schools: 12 four-year colleges and 21 community colleges.

TENNESSEE

Tennessee's BEST Prepaid Tuition Plan

888-486-BEST

www.treasury.state.tn.us/bes

Enrollment period: Open year-round.

Cost: In 2002, it will cost a lump sum of $13,804 to prepay four years of tuition and fees for a newborn.

Payment options: A single lump-sum payment, monthly payments, or you can create your own payment schedule.

State tax advantages: Not applicable (Tennessee does not have state income tax; 529 earnings are excluded from state tax interest and dividends.

Guarantee: None.

Applicable in-state, public schools: Nine four-year universities and a number of community colleges.

TEXAS

Texas Guaranteed Tuition Plan

800-445-4723

www.texastomorrowfunds.org

Enrollment period: November 1 through May 23.

Cost: In 2002, it will cost a lump sum of $17,460 (or $152 per month for 217 months) to prepay four years of tuition and fees for a newborn.

Payment options: A lump sum payment; monthly payments for 5 years, 10 years, or extended until the child reaches college age; annual payments for 5 years, 10 years, or until the child reaches college age.

State tax advantages: Texas does not have a state tax.

Guarantee: Backed by the full faith and credit of the state of Texas.

Applicable in-state, public schools: Over 100 participating colleges and universities, which include public and private, and four-year and two-year schools.

VIRGINIA

Virginia Prepaid Education Program (VPEP)

888-567-0540

www.virginia529.com

Enrollment period: February 1 through May 1.

Cost: In 2002, it cost a lump sum of $16,372 (or $140 per month for 215 months) to prepay four years of tuition and fees for a newborn.

Payment options: Prepay the full contract amount in one lump sum, make monthly payments for five years, or make monthly payments extended over the number of years until your child enters college.

State tax advantages: Contributions are deductible on your state income tax up to $2,000 per contract, with an unlimited carryover. Earnings are exempt from state income tax if the money is used (as planned) for college.

Guarantee: The governor is required to include an appropriation in the budget to over any short fall.

Applicable in-state, public schools: 16 universities and 23 community colleges.

WASHINGTON

Guaranteed Education Tuition (GET)

877-GET-TUIT

www.get.wa.gov

Enrollment period: September 15 to March 31.

Cost: In 2003, it cost a lump sum of $20,800 (or $248 per month, for 10 years) to prepay four years of tuition and fees for a newborn (rates change on September 1, 2003).

Payment options: A single lump-sum payment, customized monthly payment plan.

State tax advantages: Washington has no state income tax.

Guarantee: The plan is guaranteed by the state of Washington.

Applicable in-state, public schools: 11 four-year colleges, and 37 community and technical colleges.

WEST VIRGINIA

SMART529 Prepaid College Plan

866-574-3542

www.smart529.com

Enrollment period: To be determined.

Cost: In 2002, it cost a lump sum of $14,224 (or $164.34 per month, for 120 months) to prepay four years of tuition and fees for a newborn.

Payment options: One-time lump sum payment, a 60-month installment plan, and monthly installments over an extended period.

State tax advantages: Contributions are deductible on your state income tax. Earnings are exempt from state income tax if the money is used (as planned) for college.

Guarantee: No.

Applicable in-state, public schools: 11 universities, and 4 community colleges.

INSTITUTION-SPONSORED PREPAID TUITION PLANS

Private colleges and universities can now sponsor their own prepaid tuition plans. These plan offer all of the same benefits as state prepaid tuition plans (except that distributions will not be tax free until 2004). So, for example, if you expect junior to attend your alma mater and want to use the school's prepaid tuition plan (if they have one), contact your school for details.

To qualify as a 529 plan, the school must obtain IRS approval. To date, no schools have set up these plans.

Savings Plans

With the exception of Kentucky and Louisiana, states do not require residency for their 529 *savings* plans. From a consumer's perspective, that can be a blessing and a curse. Because you are not limited to investing in just your state's plan, that means you can shop around for the plan that best suits your needs. Isn't that a good thing? Well, yes. However, it requires a lot of legwork, and there really is no official, Morningstar-like standardized system that ranks these plans yet.

Basically, you are on your own. The personal finance magazines have all written about these plans to some degree, but the rules vary widely from plan to plan. Some plans charge commission fees, for instance, while others have residency restrictions. You really have to dig deep into the 529's literature to make sure you understand what you are getting into. (I cannot underscore this point strongly enough: You must do your homework when investigating these plans. Each state offers a different plan.) Due to space limitations, magazines just cannot cover each of these plans in-depth. Also, states are still fine-tuning their plans, so what was not available last month may be an option today.

To help you make an intelligent decision, therefore, the basic ingredients of these plans are outlined later in this chapter. Each plan's phone number and web site are listed, so you can get material sent to you. You will find that most of the 529s' literature include easy-to-read color illustrations and simple text.

Just what should you be looking for in this material? Here is what you need to know.

Investment Options

Your first reaction might be to go with the plan that offers the most options. (That is what many folks do with their retirement funds.) However, 529 plans are not 401(k)s or IRAs. You cannot easily move the money around, so it does not make that much difference how many choices you are offered because you cannot take advantage of all of them. What does matter, then? Find the one investment option that suits your needs. Some states, for instance, offer a 100 percent equity option, but not all do. Or, perhaps you like the idea of an age-based portfolio, but you feel that these investments are too conservative for your needs. You may have more of a choice here than you think. A few states, such as New York for instance, offer two different age-based portfolio tracks: The standard, more conservative ones fare as well as a more aggressive portfolio that has a greater long-term emphasis on stocks. Other states, such as Delaware and New Hampshire, let you use any of the age-based portfolios offered as your starting point, not the one that is necessarily designed for your child's age. For example: Let us say that your child is six years old. Under the plan you are considering, your investment dollars would now be allocated 80 percent to equities and 20 percent to bonds. That is the plan's position for six year olds. (As time passes, a greater portion will shift from equities to bonds.) However, you feel that approach is too conservative. Instead, you would like your money at this point to be allocated 90 percent to equities and just 10 percent to bonds. That is the plan's allocation for one year olds. If the plan allows, you may be able to start with this earlier allocation, even though your child is older. As your child ages, your asset allocation will always be a bit more aggressive than the plan intended for a child his age.

Investment Managers

Find out who is running the programs. Many of the 529s now have big-name, professional money managers, such as Salomon Smith Barney and Fidelity, managing their funds. TIAA-CREF runs the most state plans. Why is this important? These plans have not been around long enough to actually track their performance history (as you can with a regular mutual fund). It makes sense, then, to pick a 529 that is managed by a firm that at least has a history of successfully managing mutual funds and/or other investments.

Contribution Limits

All of the plans place limits on how much money can be contributed to the plan over the child's lifetime. If the plan says the maximum lifetime limit is $150,000, for example, that means you can keep making contributions to an account until the total of all the accounts (within the state's plan) for that one child reaches $150,000. Once the total hits $150,000, you cannot make any further contributions. However, plans may also have a *maximum account balance*. Once your account hits this balance, you cannot make any more contributions either. Which maximum will you hit first? It depends on how well your investments have performed and the particular limits of your plan. Let us assume that you have a maximum contribution limit of $150,000 and a maximum account balance of $250,000. You invested $125,000, and those investments really took off. Your account balance is now $250,000. You cannot make any further contributions, even though you did not actually put in the maximum contribution. Your account balance has reached its limit, so you have to stop making contributions.

Should your investments not continue to do quite so well, however, causing your account balance to fall below that $250,000 limit, you could then start making contributions again. In this case, you would only be able to contribute another $25,000 before you hit the contribution limit. At that point, you would not be able to make any further contributions, no matter what happens to your account balance, because you have hit your lifetime contribution maximum.

Your account may continue to grow, of course, far beyond the $250,000 limit. That will depend on the performance of the investment options that you have picked. Each plan creates its own total funding limits, so you must check with the particular state plan you are investing in to determine maximum contribution limits and maximum account balance limits.

How much can you contribute per year? Any individual can contribute $10,000 per year to an unlimited number of 529 plans, says Brian Orol. If you have eight children, for example, you can put $10,000, per year, into each of their 529 plans, says Orol. There is also a special gift-tax rule, explains Orol, that lets you contribute $50,000 in one year. (That same person cannot contribute any more money to the plan for a five-year period, though. The $50,000 contribution averages, then, to $10,000 per year.) These limits are per individual, so a married couple can actually make a $100,000 lump-sum contribution. This technique is used mostly by wealthy grandparents for estate planning purposes.

Taxes

Many parents will gravitate toward their state plans simply because the states offer generous tax savings. (These parents would not be wrong. It is a smart strategy to check out your home state's plan first. If it offers no tax breaks—and some states do not—then start looking at other state plans.) Some states, for example, let residents take a deduction on their state income taxes for some or all of their 529 contributions. (To qualify for this deduction, you must be a resident of the state offering the deduction, and you must invest in that state's plan.) Other states exempt earnings from income taxes. (A handful of states actually let you exempt earnings even if you invest in out-of-state plans.)

Matching Grants

A few states also offer matching grants or scholarships, based on certain restrictions, such as your income, for residents who invest in their state plan. In New Jersey, for instance, you can earn up to $1,500 in scholarship money (which can be used at a state school only) if you invest in the state plan for 12 years. In Michigan, the state matches $1 for every $3 that you invest in the first year, up to a total of $200. The restrictions? The child must be six years of age or younger, and the family cannot earn more than $80,000 annually.

ALABAMA

The Higher Education 529 Fund
866-529-2228
www.treasury.state.al.us

Minimum contribution: $250 ($25 per month with automatic contributions).

Maximum lifetime contribution: Accepts contributions until account balances reach $269,000 per student.

Investment manager: Van Kampen

Investment choices: Six

- Age-based asset allocation: Three.
- Stock: One.
- Fixed income: One.
- Other: Money market and short-term securities fun.

State tax advantages:

- Deduction: None
- Tax-free growth: Yes. You will not pay any state income tax on money withdrawn to pay qualified expenses.

Account fees: $10 annual maintenance fee ($25 for out-of-state residents). Fees are waived for accounts over $25,000.

ALASKA

University of Alaska College Savings Plan

800-478-0003

www.uacollegesavings.com

Minimum contribution: $250 ($50 if you set up an automatic investment plan).

Maximum lifetime contribution: Accepts contributions until account balances reach $250,000 per student.

Investment manager: T. Rowe Price.

Investment choices: Five options.

- Age-based asset allocation: One.
- Stock: Two.
- Fixed income: One.
- Other: One. (The Alaska College Tuition portfolio is a tuition guarantee fund. The fund guarantees that your money will grow at the same rate as tuition inflation. If not, the state of Alaska will make up the difference. This investment option is available to Alaska residents only.)

There are more investment options available under the Alaska Manulife Savings Program (minimum contributions are $500, with $50 additions).

State tax advantages: Not applicable because Alaska does not have a state income tax.

Account fees: There is a $30 annual account maintenance fee (which can be waived in certain circumstances).

ARIZONA

Arizona Family College Savings Program

800-888-2723

http://arizona.collegesavings.com

Minimum contribution: $100, $500, or $1,000, depending on which fund you invest in; you can start with $20 or $50 if you sign up for an automatic investment program.

Maximum lifetime contribution: Accepts contributions until account balances reach $187,000.

Investment manager: College Savings Bank.

Investment choices: 2 options.

- Age-based asset allocation.
- CollegSure CD.

State tax breaks:

- Deduction: None.
- Tax-free growth: Yes. You will not pay any state income tax on money withdrawn for qualified expenses.

Account fees: None.

ARKANSAS

The GiFT College Investing Plan

877-442-6553

www.thegiftplan.com

Minimum contribution: $250 for residents; $1,000 for nonresidents.

Maximum lifetime contribution: Accepts contributions until account balances reach $245,000 per student.

Investment manager: Mercury Funds.

Investment choices: Five options.

- Age-based asset allocation: One.
- Stock: Two
- Fixed income: One.
- Combination of stocks and bonds: Two.

State tax advantages:

- Deduction: None.
- Tax-free growth: Yes. You will not pay any state income tax on money withdrawn for qualified expenses.

Account fees: You will pay a $25 annual account fee. This fee is waived if you or the beneficiary is an Arkansas resident, or if your account value grows to $25,000 or more.

CALIFORNIA

Golden State ScholarShare College Savings Trust

877-728-4338

Minimum contribution: $25. You can get started with just $15, if you set up an automatic investment plan.

Maximum lifetime contribution: Accepts contributions until account balances reach $124,799 to $174,648 based on beneficiary's age.

Investment manager: TIAA-CREF.

Investment choices: Four options.

- Age-based asset allocation: Two.
- Stock: One.
- Fixed income: One.
- Other: A social choice equity option (that is, consideration is given to certain social criteria when making investment selections).

State tax breaks:

- Deduction: No.
- Tax-free growth: Yes. You will not pay any state income tax on money withdrawn for qualified expenses.

Account fees: None.

COLORADO

CollegeInvest

Scholars Choice College Savings Plan

800-478-5651 (888-572-4652 out-of-state)

Minimum contribution: $25 (subsequent contributions must be at least $15).

Maximum lifetime contribution: Accepts contributions until account balances reach $235,000 for each student.

Investment manager: Salomon Smith Barney.

Investment choices: Four options.

- Age-based asset allocation: One.
- Stock: One.
- Fixed income: One.
- Combination of stocks and bonds: One.

State tax breaks:

- Deduction: Contributions are Colorado state income tax deductible.
- Tax-free growth: Yes. You will not pay any state income tax on money withdrawn for qualified expenses.

Account fees: None, unless both you and the student are not Colorado state residents. You will then pay a $30 annual administrative fee.

CONNECTICUT

Connecticut's College Savings Program (CHET)

888-799-2438

www.aboutchet.com

Minimum contribution: $25.

Maximum lifetime contribution: Accepts contributions until account balances reach $235,000 per student.

Investment manager: TIAA-CREF.

Investment choices: Three options.

- Age-based asset allocation: One.
- Stock: One. (CHET calls one of its options *High Equity*, but it is not a pure stock fund. Here is how this portfolio is allocated: 70 percent Growth and Income Fund, 10 percent International Equity Fund, 20 percent Bond Fund.)
- Fixed income: One. (The *Principal Plus Interest* option initially invests your money in a money market fund. Eventually, those assets are allocated to an insurance product, which offers a minimum annual rate of return of 3 percent.)

State tax breaks:

- Deduction: None.
- Tax-free growth: Yes. You will not pay any state income tax on money withdrawn for qualified expenses.

Account fees: None.

DELAWARE

College Investment Plan

800-544-1655

www.fidelity.com/delaware

Minimum contribution: $500 ($50 if you sign up for an automatic investment plan).

Maximum lifetime contribution: Accepts contributions until account balances reach $250,000.

Investment manager: Fidelity.

Investment choices: Three options.

- Age-based asset allocation: One.
- Stock: One.
- Combination of stocks and bonds: One.

State tax breaks:

- Deduction: None.
- Tax-free growth: Yes, but you must pay state income tax on that money when it is withdrawn.

Account fees: An annual maintenance fee of $30. The amount is waived if you sign up for direct deposit or if your account balance exceeds $25,000.

DISTRICT OF COLUMBIA

DC 529 College Savings Program

800-987-4859

www.DCCollegeSavings.com

Minimum contribution: $100 initial ($15 with payroll deduction; $25 with automatic contribution plan); $25 subsequent contributions.

Maximum lifetime contribution: Accepts contributions until account balances reach $260,000 per student.

Investment manager: Calvert Group

Investment choices: Seven

- Age-based asset allocation: One.
- Stock: Three.
- Fixed income: One.
- Combination of stocks and bonds: One.
- Other: Guaranteed principal plus interest (minimum 3% option).

State tax advantages:

- Deduction: Contributions are deductible up to $3,000 from DC income for single filers ($6,000 for joint filers).
- Tax-free growth: Yes. You will not pay any state income tax on money withdrawn to pay qualified expenses.

Account fees: $25 enrollment fee for non-DC residents; $15 annual maintenance fee ($30 for out-of-state residents).

FLORIDA

Florida College Investment Plan

800-552-4723

www.florida529plans.com

Minimum contribution: $25 ($15 with payroll deductions or an automatic contribution plan).

Maximum lifetime contribution: Accepts contributions until account balances reach $283,000 per student.

Investment manager: Florida Prepaid College Board

Investment choices: Five

- Age-based asset allocation: One.
- Stock: Three.
- Fixed income: One.

State tax advantages: Not applicable (Florida does not have a state income tax).

Account fees: $50 enrollment fee.

GEORGIA

Georgia Higher Education Savings Plan

877-424-4377

www.gacollegeSavings.com

Minimum contribution: $25 ($15 with an automatic investment plan).

Maximum lifetime contribution: Accepts contributions until account balances reach $235,000 per student.

Investment manager: TIAA-CREF

Investment choices: Five

- Age-based asset allocation: Two.
- Stock: One.
- Combination of stocks and bonds: One.
- Other: Guaranteed fund.

State tax advantages:

- Deduction: Contributions are deductible up to $2,000 per dependent beneficiary for contributors who itemize on their federal income tax returns and have AGI under $100,000 on a joint return or $50,000 for single or separate filers.
- Tax-free growth: Yes. You will not pay any state income tax on money withdrawn to pay qualified expenses (but there is no exemption for funds withdrawn within the first year).

Account fees: None.

HAWAII

TuitionEDGE

643-4529 in-state; 866-529-3343 out-of-state

www.tuitionedge.com

Minimum contribution: $15 per investment option.

Maximum lifetime contribution: Accepts contributions until account balances reach $253,000 per student.

Investment manager: Delaware Investments

Investment choices: Five.

- Age-based asset allocation: One.
- Stock: Two.
- Combination of stocks and bonds: One.
- Other: Savings account with First Hawaiian Bank.

State tax advantages:

- Deduction: None.
- Tax-free growth: Yes. You will not pay any state income tax on money withdrawn to pay qualified expenses.

Account fees: $25 annual maintenance fee (waived for accounts over $10,000 and for HI residents).

IDAHO

Idaho College Savings Program (IDeal)

866-433-2533

www.idsaves.org

Minimum contribution: $25 ($15 if you sign up for an automatic investment plan.)

Maximum lifetime contribution: Accepts contributions until account balances reach $235,000 per student.

Investment manager: TIAA-CREF.

Investment choices: Three options.

- Age-based asset allocation: One.
- Stock: One.
- Other: One (a guaranteed option will be invested in the TIAA-CREF Institutional Money Market Fund).

State tax advantages:

- Deduction: You can deduct contributions up to a maximum of $4,000 per individual taxpayer. (For joint filers, it is $8,000.)
- Tax-free growth: Yes. You are not taxed on money withdrawn for qualified expenses.

Account fees: None.

ILLINOIS

Bright Start College Savings Program

877-432-7444

www.brightstartsavings.com

Minimum contribution: $25 ($15, if you set up an automatic investment plan).

Maximum lifetime contribution: Accepts contributions until account balances reach $235,000 per student.

Investment manager: Salomon Smith Barney.

Investment choices: Six options.

- Age-based asset allocation: Two.
- Stock: One.
- Fixed income: Three.

State tax breaks:

- Deduction: Unlimited for original contributions.
- Tax-free growth: Yes. You will not pay any state income tax on money withdrawn for qualified expenses.

Account fees: One-time $30 enrollment fee (more if account is opened through a bank).

INDIANA

CollegeChoice 529 Plan

866-400-7526

www.collegechoiceplan.com

Minimum contribution: $50 initial; subsequent at least $25.

Maximum lifetime contribution: Accepts contributions until account balances reach $114,548 per student (increasing to $236,750).

Investment manager: OneGroup Investments.

Investment choices: Eight options.

- Age-based asset allocation: One.
- Stock: Four.
- Fixed income: Two.
- Combination of stocks and bonds: One.

State tax breaks:

- Deduction: None.
- Tax-free growth: Yes. You will not pay state income taxes on that money withdrawn for qualified expenses.

Account fees: There is a $10 annual fee ($30 for non-resident accounts).

IOWA

College Savings Iowa

888-672-9116

www.collegesavingsiowa.com

Minimum contribution: $25 (but total contributions for the year must be at least $50).

Maximum lifetime contribution: Accepts contributions until account balance reaches $239,000 per student.

Investment manager: Vanguard.

Investment choices: Four options.

- Age-based asset allocation: Four.

   (There are four different age-based portfolios: growth, moderate growth, conservative growth, and income.)

State tax breaks:

- Deduction: Contributions up to $2180 per account are deductible from Iowa income taxes. (The amount is adjusted annually for inflation.)
- Tax-free growth: Yes. You do not pay state income tax on that money withdrawn for qualified expenses.

Account fees: None.

KANSAS

Learning Quest Education Savings Program

800-579-2203

www.learningquestsavings.com

Minimum contribution: $2,500 ($500 if you are a Kansas resident). You can start with just $50 ($25 if you are a Kansas resident), if you set up a regular, monthly investment account.

Maximum lifetime contribution: Accepts contributions until account balance reaches $235,000 per student.

Investment manager: American Century.

Investment choices: Three.

- Age-based asset allocation: Three.

  There are three diversified investment tracks based on risk tolerance: aggressive, moderate, and conservative. Within each investment track, there are six portfolios tailored to the child's age.

State tax breaks:

- Deduction: Kansas taxpayers receive an annual adjusted gross income deduction of up to $2,000 ($4,000 if married filing jointly) for contributions made to the program. The deduction is allowed per student, per year.
- Tax-free growth: Yes. You will not pay state income tax on the money withdrawn to pay qualified expenses.

Account fees: $40 per year. The fee is just $10, however, if you are a Kansas resident, an American Century Priority Investor, or your account value is more than $100,000.

KENTUCKY

Kentucky Education Savings Plan Trust

877-598-7878

www.kentuckytrust.org

Minimum contribution: $25 ($15, if you sign up for an automatic investment plan).

Maximum lifetime contribution: $235,000 per student.

Investment manager: TIAA-CREF.

Investment choices: Two options.

- Age-based asset allocation: One.
- Stock: One.

State tax breaks:

- Deduction: None.
- Tax-free growth: Yes. You will not pay any state income tax when money is used for qualified expenses.

Account fees: None.

LOUISIANA

Student Tuition Assistance and Revenue Trust Program (START)

800-259-5626

www.osfa.state.la.us/START.h

Minimum contribution: $10.

Maximum lifetime contribution: $173,065 per student (the amount changes annually).

Investment manager: State Treasurer.

Investment choices: One option.

- Fixed income: One.

Please note: The plan has been authorized by the state legislature to offer additional variable investments, such as equities and bonds, but at press time, these investment options were not yet available.

State tax breaks:

- Deduction: You can deduct up to $2,400 of your annual contributions from Louisiana state taxable income.
- Tax-free growth: Yes. You will not pay any state income tax when money is used for qualified expenses.

Account fees: None.

MAINE

NextGen College Investing Plan (NextGen)

877-463-9843

www.nextgenplan.com

Minimum contribution: $250 ($50, if you sign up for an automatic monthly savings plan).

Maximum lifetime contribution: $153,000 per student.

Investment manager: Merrill Lynch.

Investment choices: Four options.

- Age-based asset allocation: One.
- Stock: One.
- Fixed income: One.
- Combination of stocks and bonds: One.
- Other: If you open your account through a Merrill Lynch broker you can pick from 11 different investment options, offered through four different fund families.

State tax breaks:

- Deduction: None.
- Tax-free growth: Yes. You will not pay any state income tax when money is used (as planned) for higher education.

Account fees: An annual account maintenance fee of $50 (waived in certain circumstances).

MARYLAND

College Investment Plan

888-463-4723

www.collegesavingsmd.org

Minimum contribution: $250 ($25 if you set up an automatic investment plan).

Maximum lifetime contribution: $175,000 per student.

Investment manager: T. Rowe Price.

Investment choices: Four.

- Age-based asset allocation: One.
- Stock: One.
- Fixed income: One.
- Combination of stocks and bonds: One.

State tax advantages:

- Deduction: The amount you contribute each year can be deducted from your Maryland state taxable income, up to a maximum of $2,500 *per student*, per year. Payments in excess of $2,500 can be deducted per student can be carried forward for up to 10 years.
- Tax-free growth: Yes. You will not pay any state income tax when money is used for qualified expenses.

Account fees: $90 enrollment (reduced under certain conditions); $30 annual fee.

MASSACHUSETTS

Fund College Investing Plan

800-544-2776

www.mefa.org

Minimum contribution: $1,000 ($50, if you set up an automatic investment account).

Maximum lifetime contribution: $230,000 per student.

Investment manager: Fidelity.

Investment choices: Three options.

- Age-based asset allocation: One.
- Stock: One.
- Combination of stocks and bonds: One.

State tax breaks:

- Deduction: None.
- Tax-free growth: Yes. You will not pay state income tax on money withdrawn for qualified expenses.

Account fees: An annual fee of $30. This fee is waived if you sign up for a systematic payment plan or if your account balance is $25,000 or more.

MICHIGAN

The Michigan Education Savings Program (MESP)

877-861-6377

www.misaves.com

Minimum contribution: $25 ($15, if you set up an automatic investment plan).

Maximum lifetime contribution: Accepts contributions until account balances reach $235,000 per student.

Investment manager: TIAA-CREF.

Investment choices: Three options.

- Age-based asset allocation: One.
- Stock: One.
- Other: One (a guaranteed option that invests initially in the TIAA-CREF Institutional Money Market Fund).

State tax advantages:

- Deduction: You can deduct up to $5,000 of your annual contributions from Michigan state taxable income ($10,000 for married couples filing jointly).
- Tax-free growth: Yes. You will not pay any state income tax when money is used for qualified expenses.

Account fees: None.

MINNESOTA

Minnesota College Savings Plan

877-338-4646

www.mnsaves.org

Minimum contribution: $25 ($15 for payroll deduction deposit).

Maximum lifetime contribution: Accepts contributions until account balances reach $235,000 per student.

Investment manager: TIAA-CREF.

Investment choices: Three options.

- Age-based asset allocation: One.
- Stock: One.
- Other: One (a guaranteed option)

State tax advantages:

- Deduction: None.
- Tax-free growth: Yes. You will not pay any state income tax when money is used for qualified expenses.

Account fees: None.

MISSISSIPPI

Mississippi Affordable College Savings Program (MACS)

800-486-3670

www.collegesavingsms.com

Minimum contribution: $25 ($15 if you set up an automatic investment plan).

Maximum lifetime contribution: Accepts contributions until account balances reach $235,000 per student.

Investment manager: TIAA-CREF.

Investment choices: Three options.

- Age-based asset allocation: One.
- Stock: One.
- Fixed income: One.
- Other: If you open your account through the Advisor Program there are seven TIAA-CREF mutual funds, plus one guaranteed investment option.

State tax breaks:

- Deduction: The amount you contribute each year can be deducted from your Mississippi taxable income up to a maximum of $10,000 per individual (up to $20,000 for joint filers).
- Tax-free growth: Yes. You will not pay any state income tax when money is used for qualified expenses.

Account fees: None.

MISSOURI

Missouri Saving For Tuition Program (MO$T)

888-414-6678

www.missourimost.org

Minimum contribution: $25 ($15 if you set up an automatic investment plan).

Maximum lifetime contribution: Accepts contributions until account balances reach $235,000 per student.

Investment manager: TIAA-CREF.

Investment choices: Three options.

- Age-based asset allocation: One.
- Stock: One.
- Other: A guaranteed option that guarantees principal and a minimum interest rate of 3 percent.

Also, if you open your account through the Advisor Program, there are seven TIAA-CREF mutual funds, plus one guaranteed investment option.

State tax breaks:

- Deduction: You can deduct up to $8,000 of your contributions per year from your Missouri state taxable income.
- Tax-free growth: Yes. You will not pay any state income tax when money is used for qualified expenses.

Account fees: None.

MONTANA

Montana Family Education Savings Program

800-888-2723

http://montana.collegesavings.com

Minimum contribution: $250 ($25 with payroll deduction deposits; $100 per month or $250 per quarter for automatic bank transfers).

Maximum lifetime contribution: Cumulative contribution is currently limited to $187,000.

Investment manager: College Savings Bank
Investment choices: One

- Other: Certificate of deposit with maturities ranging from one to 25 years. Note: Montana also offers a college savings plan through Pacific Life with 14 mutual funds and 5 asset allocation options.

State tax advantages:

- Deduction: Contributions are deductible up to $3,000 per year for single filers ($6,000 for joint filers).
- Tax-free growth: Yes. You will not pay any state income tax on money withdrawn to pay qualified expenses.

Account fees: None.

NEBRASKA

College Savings Plan of Nebraska

888-993-3746

www.planforcollegenow.com

Minimum contribution: None.

Maximum lifetime contribution: $235,000 per student.

Investment manager: Union Bank & Trust.

Investment choices: 10 options.

- Age-based asset allocation: Four.
- Stock: One.
- Fixed income: One.
- Combination of stocks and bonds: Four.

State tax advantages:

- Deduction: Residents can take an income tax deduction of up to $1,000 per tax return ($500 for married couples filing separately).
- Tax-free growth: Yes. You will not pay any state income tax when money is used for qualified expenses.

Account fees: There is an annual account maintenance fee of $20.

NEW HAMPSHIRE

UNIQUE College Investing Plan

800-544-1722

www.Fidelity.com/unique

Minimum contribution: $1,000 ($50, if you set up an automatic investment program).

Maximum lifetime contribution: $233,240 per student.

Investment manager: Fidelity.

Investment choices: Four options.

- Age-based asset allocation: One.
- Stock: Two.
- Fixed income: Zero.
- Combination of stocks and bonds: One.

State tax breaks:

- Deduction: None (New Hampshire does not have an income tax).
- Tax-free growth: Not applicable (New Hampshire does not have an income tax).

Account fees: An annual maintenance fee of $30 per year. The fee is waived if you sign up for direct deposit or if your account balance exceeds $25,000.

Residency: Not Required.'

NEW JERSEY

New Jersey Better Educational Savings Trust (NJBEST)

877-4NJBEST

www.hesaa.org/students/njbes

Minimum contribution: $25 per month, or $300 per year, up to $1,200.

Maximum lifetime contribution: $185,000 per student.

Investment manager: The Division of Investment at the New Jersey Department of the Treasury.

Investment choices: One option.

- Age-based asset allocation: One.

State tax breaks:

- Deduction: None.
- Tax-free growth: Yes. You will not pay any state income tax when money is used for qualified expenses.

Account fees: There is an annual account fee of $5.

Residency: Required. You or the student must be a New Jersey resident.

NEW MEXICO

The Education Plan's College Savings Program

877-EDPLANS

www.theeducationplan.com

Minimum contribution: $250 ($25, if you invest through an automatic monthly plan).

Maximum lifetime contributions: Accepts contributions until account balances reach $251,000 per student.

Investment manager: Schoolhouse Capital, a subsidiary of State Street Corporation.

Investment choices: Nine options.

- Age-based asset allocation: One.
- Stock: One.
- Fixed income: Two.
- Combination of stocks and bonds: Five.

State tax breaks:

- Deduction: All contributions are state income tax deductible.
- Tax-free growth: Yes. You will not pay any state income tax when money is used for qualified expenses.

Account fees: A $30 annual account maintenance fee. This fee is waived if you contribute with automatic contributions through your checking account, or if you are a New Mexico resident and have an account balance of at least $10,000.

Residency: Not Required.

NEW YORK

New York's College Savings Program

877-697-2837

www.nysaves.org

Minimum contribution: $25 ($15 per pay period for payroll deduction accounts).

Maximum lifetime contribution: $100,000 per student (or until account balances reach $235,000).

Investment manager: TIAA-CREF.

Investment choices: Four options.

- Age-based asset allocation: Two.
- Stock: One.
- Other: A guaranteed option that invests in a variety of fixed income investments.

State tax breaks:

- Deduction: You can deduct up to $5,000 of your annual contributions from your New York State taxable income ($10,000 for married couples filing jointly).
- Tax-free growth: Yes. You will not pay any state income tax when money is used for qualified expenses.

Account fees: None.

Residency: Not Required.

NORTH CAROLINA

North Carolina's National College Savings Program

800-600-3453

www.cfnc.org/savings

Minimum contribution: $50.

Maximum lifetime contribution: Accepts contributions until account balances reach $268,804 per student.

Investment manager: College Foundation Inc..

Investment choices: Six options.

- Age-based asset allocation: One.
- Stock: One
- Fixed income: One
- Combination of stocks and bonds: One
- Other: Choice of 22 portfolios in the Seligman CollegeHorizons Fund

State tax breaks:

- Deduction: None.
- Tax-free growth: Yes. You will not pay any North Carolina state income tax when you withdraw the money if the money is used (as planned) for higher education.

Account fees: None.

Residency: Required. You or the child must be a resident or employed in-state.

NORTH DAKOTA

College SAVE

800-728-3529

www.collegesave4U.com

Minimum contribution: $300 during the first year ($25, if you set up an automatic monthly investment plan).

Maximum lifetime contribution: $168,000 per student.

Investment manager: Morgan Stanley.

Investment choices: Seven options.

- Age-based asset allocation: Three.
- Stock: Two.
- Combination of stocks and bonds: Two.

State tax advantages:

- Deduction: None.
- Tax-free growth: Yes. You will not pay any state income tax when money is used for qualified expenses.

Account fees: You will pay an annual account fee of $30 unless you are a resident of North Dakota.

Residency: Not Required.

OHIO

CollegeAdvantage Savings Plan

800-233-6734

www.collegeadvantage.com

Minimum contribution: $15.

Maximum lifetime contribution: Accepts contributions until account balances reach $232,000 per student.

Investment manager: Putnam Investments.

Investment choices: Five options.

- Age-based asset allocation: One.
- Stock: One.
- Combination of stocks and bonds: Two.
- Other: One (Guaranteed Savings Fund).

State tax advantages:

- Deduction: You can deduct up to $2,000 of your annual contributions per beneficiary from your Ohio State taxable income, with unlimited carryforwards of excess contributions. (The amount is the same for single filers and married couples filing jointly.)

- Tax-free growth: Yes. You will not pay any state income tax when money is used for qualified expenses.

Account fees: You will pay an annual account maintenance fee of $25 for all variable investments (that is all the investment options listed previously, except the guaranteed savings fund). The fee will be waived, however, if you set up an automatic investment plan of at least $50 per month, or if your account balance exceeds $25,000.

Residency: Not Required. But there are two different versions of the savings plan. One for residents, one for non-residents. (Non-residents, for example, cannot invest in the guaranteed savings fund.)

OKLAHOMA

Oklahoma College Savings Plan

877-654-7284

www.ok4saving.org

Minimum contribution: $25 ($15 per pay period for payroll deduction deposits).

Maximum lifetime contribution: Accepts contributions until account balances reach $235,000 per student.

Investment manager: TIAA-CREF.

Investment choices: Three options.

- Age-based asset allocation: One.
- Stock: One.
- Other: One (a guaranteed option that invests initially in money-market funds).

State tax advantages:

- Deduction: You can deduct up to $2,500 per student (up to $10,000 per tax-payer) of your annual contributions from your Oklahoma state taxable income.
- Tax-free growth: Yes. You will not pay any state income tax when money is used for qualified expenses.

Account fees: None.

Residency: Not Required.

OREGON

Oregon College Savings Plan

866-772-8464

www.OregonCollegeSavings.com

Minimum contribution: $250 (you can start with just $25 when you set up an automatic investment plan).

Maximum lifetime contribution: Accepts contributions until account balances reach $250,000 per student.

Investment manager: Strong Capital Management.

Investment choices: Seven options.

- Age-based asset allocation: One.
- Stock: One.
- Combination of stocks and bonds: Five.

State tax breaks:

- Deduction: You can deduct up to $2,000 in annual contributions from your state income taxes. (If you are married filing separately, it is $1,000.)
- Tax-free growth: Yes. You will not pay any state income tax when money is used for qualified expenses.

Account fees: None.

Residency: Required.

PENNSYLVANIA

TAP 529 Investment Plan

800-440-4000

www.lfg.com/LincolnPageServe

Minimum contribution: $1,000 initial; $50 subsequent contributions.

Maximum lifetime contribution: Accepts contributions until account balances reach $290,000 per student.

Investment manager: Delaware Investments

Investment choices: Nine

- Age-based asset allocation: Two.
- Stock: Five.
- Fixed income: One.
- Combination of stocks and bonds: One.

State tax advantages:

- Deduction: None.
- Tax-free growth: Yes. You will not pay any state income tax on money withdrawn to pay qualified expenses.

Account fees: $25 annual maintenance fee (waived for accounts over $20,000 or with payroll deduction or automatic contributions).

RHODE ISLAND

CollegeBound*fund*

888-324-5057

www.collegeboundfund.com

Minimum contribution: $1,000; subsequent contributions must be at least $50.

Maximum lifetime contribution: Accepts contributions until account balances reach $287,070 per student.

Investment manager: Alliance Capital.

Investment choices: Five options.

- Age-based asset allocation: Two.
- Stock: Two (an aggressive growth portfolio that invests in aggressive growth equity funds, including technology and international funds, and a growth portfolio that invests in equity funds that are not as aggressive as the previous option).
- Combination of stocks and bonds: One (invests in a set mix of 60 percent equity funds and 40 percent fixed income funds).

State tax breaks:

- Deduction: You can deduct $500 ($1,000 in a joint return) against Rhode Island income, with a carryover of the expense to future years.
- Tax-free growth: Yes, You will not pay state income tax on money withdrawn for qualified expenses.

Account fees: There is an annual account fee of $25 (waived for accounts with a balance of at least $25,000 and accounts funded through an automatic contribution plan or payroll deductions).

Residency: Not Required.

SOUTH CAROLINA

Future Scholar 529 College Savings Plan

888-244-5674

www.futurescholar.com

Minimum contribution: $250 initial; $50 subsequent contributions.

Maximum lifetime contribution: Accepts contributions until account balances reach $250,000 per student.

Investment manager: Banc of America Advisors LLC

Investment choices: Ten

- Age-based asset allocation: One.
- Stock: Two.
- Fixed income: One.
- Other: Instead of selecting individual funds, you may choose from six allocation portfolios (aggressive growth, growth, balanced growth, balanced, income and growth and income).

State tax advantages:

- Deduction: Contributions are fully deductible.
- Tax-free growth: Yes. You will not pay any state income tax on money withdrawn to pay qualified expenses.

Account fees: $25 enrollment fee and $25 annual maintenance fee (each of which is waived for in-state residents).

SOUTH DAKOTA

CollegeAccess 529

866-529-7462

www.CollegeAccess529.com

Minimum contribution: $250 initial ($50 per month through an automatic investment plan.

Maximum lifetime contribution: Accepts contributions until account balances reach $305,000 per student.

Investment manager: PIMCO Funds

Investment choices: 23

- Age-based asset allocation: One.
- Fixed income: One.
- Other: You can select from 16 individual funds and 5 customized portfolios (capital appreciation, core equity, total return plus, real return plus, and money market plus), through Advisor-sold accounts.

State tax advantages: Not applicable (South Dakota does not have an income tax).

Account fees: None.

TENNESSEE

BEST Savings Plan

888-486-BEST

www.tnbest.org

Minimum contribution: $25 ($15 if you set up an automatic monthly investment program).

Maximum lifetime contribution: Accepts contributions until account balances reach $235,000 per student.

Investment manager: TIAA-CREF.

Investment choices: Two option.

- Age-based asset allocation: One.
- Stock: One.

State tax breaks: Not applicable (Tennessee does not have state income tax and 592 earnings are exempt from state tax on interest and dividends).

Account fees: None.

Residency: Not Required.

TEXAS

Tomorrow's College Investment Plan

800-445-GRAD

www.texastomorrowfunds.org

Minimum contribution: $25 ($15 with payroll deduction and automatic contribution plans).

Maximum lifetime contribution: Accepts contributions until account balances reach $257,460 per student.

Investment manager: Enterprise Capital Management

Investment choices: 16

- Age-based asset allocation: One.
- Stock: Nine.
- Fixed income: Three.
- Combination of stocks and bonds: One.
- Other: You can also select from two allocation portfolios (100% stock allocation and balanced allocation).

State tax advantages: Not applicable (Texas does not have an income tax).

Account fees: $30 annual maintenance fee (waived for in-state residents and automatic purchase plans, payroll deduction plans and accounts with balances of $25,000 or more).

UTAH

Utah Educational Savings Plan Trust (UESP)

800-418-2551

www.uesp.org

Minimum contribution: $25 per month—must contribute at least $300 per year.

Maximum lifetime contribution: Accepts contributions until account balances reach $260,000 per statement.

Investment manager: The state of Utah invests in the Utah State Treasurer's Investment Fund (that is the money market option); the other three portfolios are invested in Vanguard funds.

Investment choices: Five options.

- Age-based asset allocation: Two.
- Stock: One.
- Fixed income: One.
- Other: One. (State Treasurer's Fund, which is fixed income plus a share of endowment fund earnings).

State tax breaks:

- Deduction: Contributions up to $1,410 for 2002 ($2,820 for joint filers) are exempt from Utah state income tax. (The maximum deductible contribution amount is adjusted annually for inflation.)
- Tax-free growth: Yes. You will not pay any Utah state income tax when money is used (as planned) for college.

Account fees: You are charged an annual account fee of $5 (per thousand dollars invested), up to a maximum of $25. (This fee does not apply to the fixed income investment option.)

Residency: Not Required.

VERMONT

Higher Education Savings Plan

800-637-5860

www.vsac.org

Minimum contribution: $25 ($15 if you set up an automatic monthly investment program).

Maximum lifetime contribution: Accepts contributions until account balances reach $240,000 per student.

Investment manager: TIAA-CREF.

Investment choices: Four options.

- Age-based asset allocation: Two.
- Stock: One.
- Fixed income: One.

State tax breaks:

- Deduction: None.
- Tax-free growth: Yes. You will not pay any state income tax when money is used (as planned) for college.

Account fees: None.

Residency: Not required.

VIRGINIA

Virginia Education Savings Trust (VEST)

888-567-0540

www.virginia529.com

Minimum contribution: $25.

Maximum lifetime contribution: Accepts contributions until account balances reach $250,000 per student.

Investment manager: Virginia College Savings Plan Board.

Investment choices: Five options.

- Age-based asset allocation: One.
- Stock: Three.
- Fixed income: One.

Other: Under Virginia's College America plan, sold exclusively through financial advisers, there are 21 fund options.

State tax breaks:

- Deduction: You can deduct up to $2,000 of your contributions per year on your Virginia state income tax.
- Tax-free growth: Yes. You will not pay any state income tax when money is used (as planned) for higher education.

Account fees: There is an application fee of $85.

Residency: Not Required.

WASHINGTON

Plan under development and will launch in mid-2003.

WEST VIRGINIA

SMART 529 College Savings Option

866-574-3542

www.smart529.com

Minimum contribution: $100 and $15 subsequent or $15 per month (higher for broker-sold plan).

Maximum lifetime contribution: Accepts contributions until account balances reach $265,620 per student.

Investment manager: Hartford Life

Investment choices: Five

- Age-based asset allocation: One.
- Stock: Two.
- Fixed income: One.
- Combination of stocks and bonds: One.
- Other: 8 additional funds options through broker-sold plans.

State tax advantages:

- Deduction: Contributions are fully deductible for West Virginia residents.
- Tax-free growth: Yes. You will not pay any state income tax on money withdrawn to pay qualified expenses.

Account fees: $25 (waived for WV residents, automatic contribution accounts, and accounts over $25,000).

WISCONSIN

EdVest College Savings Program

888-338-3789

www.EDVEST.com

Minimum contribution: $250 ($25 when you set up an automatic investment plan).

Maximum lifetime contribution: Accepts contributions until account balances reach $246,000 per student.

Investment manager: Strong Capital Management.

Investment choices: Six options.

- Age-based asset allocation: One.
- Stock: One.
- Fixed income: One.
- Combination of stocks and bonds: Three.

State tax advantages:

- Deduction: You can deduct up to $3,000 of your annual contributions from your Wisconsin state taxable income.
- Tax-free growth: Yes. You will not pay any state income tax when money is used (as planned) for higher education.

Account fees: You will be charged a $10 enrollment fee and a $10 annual fee (waived in certain circumstances).

Residency: Not Required.

WYOMING

College Achievement Plan

877-529-2655

www.collegeachievementplan.com

Minimum contribution: $250 ($1,000 for nonresident).

Maximum lifetime contribution: Accepts contributions until account balances reach $245,000 per student.

Investment manager: Mercury Advisors.

Investment choices: Five options.

- Age-based asset allocation: One.
- Stock: One.
- Fixed income: One.
- Combination of stocks and bonds: Two.

State tax breaks: Not applicable in this case because Wyoming does *not* have a tax.

Account fees: There is an annual account maintenance fee of $50 (waived if either you or the student are a Wyoming resident or account balance is $25,000 or more).

Residency: Not Required.

CHAPTER 5

Getting Professional Help

Setting up a college savings plan can be overwhelming. There are so many choices to pick from and ultimately, so many decisions to be made.

Even if you have worked out how much money you need to save and how you are actually going to budget for those savings, you still need to make many other important decisions, such as how that money will be invested, the tax consequences of those investments, in whose name the money should be invested, and how that investment portfolio should change over time.

Take bonds, for example. A bond is just one type of investment that you might want to consider for some of your college savings. Yet, making an intelligent decision to invest in bonds involves more than hearing a sales pitch on the radio while you are showering one morning and saying, "Gee, I think I will buy bonds for little Stevie." Before you can make the decision to invest in a bond, you need to understand what a bond is, how it works, what type of return you can expect, and the various types of bonds available, such as a municipal bond, a triple-tax free bond, a savings bond, and a baccalaureate bond.

Of course, you can learn about bonds (and stocks, certificates of deposit [CDs], and most other types of investments) by reading books and magazine articles. The personal finance shelves at bookstores are overflowing with how-to books on every aspect of saving, spending, and investing. The major business and finance magazines like *Kiplinger's* and *Money* regularly devote special issues to the best mutual funds. Do-it-yourself investors also can educate themselves by surfing the web. The Internet is loaded with free, financial information that you can access quickly and easily.

However, many people simply do not have the time and/or the inclination to wade through this mountain of material. Not all of the information that you read is useful. Some of it may even be misleading or wrong, and learning about investments is not the do-it-yourself investor's sole task. You must then make appropriate investments, track the progress of those investments, decide when to buy and sell those investments *and* still take care of children, manage a home, socialize with friends and family, exercise, pursue hobbies, read an occasional book or magazine, and go to work.

That is where a financial planner comes in. A financial planner, as the name suggests, is a professional who knows all about, well, planning your finances. Seriously, he or she is well-versed in money and how to manage it. That includes everything from budgets, personal debt issues, and cash flow concerns to investment options, retirement planning, and college savings plans. Ah, yes. You need to save money for Elizabeth's college education? Most financial planners can help you build a college fund by a) plotting a strategy for savings, b) picking appropriate investments to reach those goals, and c) helping you stay on track with those savings.

Good financial planners offer more than investment advice, though. A planner can help navigate you through tough times. If the Dow Jones Industrial Average is in a slump (and stock prices fall), a planner can often help you from overreacting. Some investors, for example, sell at the first sign of a downturn. However, most financial planners will tell you—hold your hand even, if necessary—that markets go up and down. You simply have to wait out the bad periods. Many go-it-alone investors lose money, in fact, by jumping in and out of the market, says the Financial Planning Association (FPA). Naturally, you will not be immune to slumping markets if you use a financial planner rather than doing it yourself. However, most financial planning clients maintain a much more diversified portfolio, says the FPA, so their investments are not hit as hard when a particular sector, such as tech stocks or the market at large, tumbles.

You will have to pay for this guidance, of course. How much you will pay and what type of service you receive will depend on the type of financial planner that you select.

Who's Who in Financial Planning?

Unlike most other professions, the financial planning industry is largely unregulated. Planners do not need a degree in financial planning (or in any other subject, for that matter), a passing grade on a certification exam, or some experience in the field to set up shop. Anyone, in fact, can hang out a financial planning shingle and offer his or her professional services, but what does that mean? What kind of service? There are no real standards, so all financial planners will not offer the same services or capabilities. In this degree-rich society that we live in, that may be surprising and somewhat disappointing. How can you find a reputable financial planner if you have no guidelines, no Good Housekeeping Seal of Approval so to speak, to measure with?

Fortunately, the financial planning industry does grant certain designations or certifications that are widely-respected and that tell you something about a planner's formal training in investing and money management and his or her on-the-job experience. These designations are not mandatory, though, so do not assume that all financial planners satisfy these requirements just because they call themselves financial planning professionals. The most common credentials, which you will usually find written after a planner's name, much like a medical doctor does with an M.D., are as follows.

Certified Financial Planner (CFP)

The Certified Financial Planner Board of Standards, a nonprofit professional regulatory organization, was founded in 1985. The board awards its trademark designation—the most well-known of such designations by consumers—to individuals who meet the board's rigorous requirements. (The board itself is accredited by the National Commission for Certifying Agencies, which is the accrediting body of the Washington-DC–based National Organization for Competency Assurance.)

To become a CFP, you must master more than 100 integrated financial planning topics, such as budgeting, bond and stock valuation methods, and estate planning through an approved study course, pass a 10-hour, comprehensive exam, adhere to a code of professional ethics, log three years of relevant experience (if you do not have a college degree, you need five years of experience), and complete 30 hours of continuing education courses every two years. For information about requirements, you can contact the board at 888-CFP-MARK or *www.cfp-board.org*.

The former designation of Chartered Financial Consultant (CHFC) is no longer offered. The American College in Bryn Mawr, Pennsylvania also awards this designation. For more, contact the college at 888-263-7265 or *www. amercoll.edu*.

Personal Financial Specialist (PFS)

This financial planning specialty accreditation by the American Institute of Certified Public Accountants (AICPA) is given exclusively to certified public accountants who are trained in personal finance (and who are members of the AICPA). Recipients will have passed a six-hour test, have experience in six areas of financial planning (goal setting, estate planning, investment planning, risk management, income tax planning, and retirement planning), will take some continuing education courses, and must reapply for this accreditation every three years. Keep in mind that PFSs will have already passed the strict requirements needed for a CPA, too: namely, a college degree in accounting, two years of experience working at a public accounting firm, and a passing grade on the four-part CPA exam. The AICPA created the PFS credential in 1987. For more information contact the AICPA at 888-777-70077 or *www.aicpa.org.*

You can also check with the National Association of Securities Dealers Registration (301-590-6500, *www.nasd.com*). Agents who sell stocks, bonds, and mutual funds (that would be commission-based planners and most fee-based planners) must also be *registered investment advisors*. If you are interested, you can also ask NASD if there have been any complaints or disciplinary action filed against the financial planner.

Fees and Service

You will find a lot of planners ready to give you advice. One smart way to distinguish one planner from another, however, is to find out how they are paid. That will tell you a lot about the kind of service you can expect and how much you can expect to pay them.

Fee-Only Planners

You pay this planner for her financial advice—period. Let us say that you need help setting up a college fund for your 10-year-old daughter. A fee-only planner will look at your income, savings and other assets, and then show you ways to reach your financial goal. For this service, she will probably charge you an hourly rate (about $100 to $150 per hour, on average), an annual fee (0.5 to 1.5 percent of your portfolio), or a flat fee per year. She may recommend investments by name, but she will never earn a commission for selling you a particular mutual fund. Often, in fact, fee-only planners recommend funds that are no-loads (which means you do not pay a sales charge). The advantage to this type of service: Because fee-only planners do not earn commissions on products sold, it is more likely that their recommendations will be made in your best interest.

Commission-Based Planners

This adviser *does* receive a commission for products sold. He will give you advice (much like a fee-only planner), but he will also sell you the products. That can be good and bad. The good news is that a commission-based planner does not charge you for advice (so it will cost you less out-of-pocket), and you do not have to look elsewhere for someone to help you buy the products. The bad news is that this planner gets paid from the mutual fund companies, banks, and insurance companies when he sells their investment products. That means he earns money only when you buy a product that he is selling. *Hmmm.* Is he unbiased? Is he truly suggesting the best investment for you? Or is he merely touting the investment that will earn him the biggest commission? In addition, a commission-based planner will not charge outright for his advice, but you will pay for it through your investments. Sales charges (or loads) are ultimately deducted from your investment.

Fee-Based Planners

This adviser is a chameleon: Depending on the situation, he may charge a fee (like a fee-only planner) or a commission (like a commission-based planner).

Finding a Financial Planner

The best way to find any type of professional—be it a doctor, a lawyer, or a financial planner—is through a personal recommendation. Ask friends, colleagues, and relatives (especially those with college-bound kids), and even other professionals that you work with, such as your lawyer or accountant, if they know a planner that they would recommend. You want the name of the planner, for instance, who did work for your Uncle Joe *if* your Uncle Joe was happy with the service and *if* your financial situation is similar to Uncle Joe's. Most financial planners can advise you about the more common personal finance issues. College planning, for example, is a staple for most, but planners also specialize in one or two specific areas. Obviously, you do not want a retirement specialist if you are interested in college planning (unless you are nearing retirement age and worried, perhaps, that funding your son's tuition will derail your retirement savings). Still, you want a planner who can help you devise a solid college savings strategy now, and then, when the time comes, help you unravel the mystery of the financial aid process.

If you cannot find any good candidates through personal recommendation, then you will have to find one via the professional association route. The following organizations will supply you with the names of financial planners in your area if you write, call, or visit them on their web sites:

- To find a fee-only planner, contact The Garrett Planning Network at 866-260-88400, *www.GarrettPlanningNetwork.com*. The site's geographic locator will pull up the files (including background and pictures) of planners in your area.
- To find a fee-only planner, contact the National Association of Personal Financial Advisors at 888-FEE-ONLY, *www.napfa.org*.
- To find a financial planner who specializes in college planning, contact the Academy of College Financial Planning's web site at *www.academy ofcollwegefinancialplanning.org*. You will find the names of qualified college financial planning professionals who have demonstrated a level of knowledge that meets standards set by the academy's board of directors.
- For the names of certified financial planners, chartered life underwriters (they can sell life, disability, and long-term care insurance), and other

financial planners in your area, contact the Society of Financial Service Professionals at 270 South Bryn Mawr Avenue, Bryn Mawr, PA 19010, 610-526-2500, *www.financialpro.org* (look under consumer referral.) The society, which is the nation's oldest and largest organization of credentialed insurance and financial advisors with 30,000 members nationwide, will send you the names of up to five members in your area, plus a free brochure with tips about personal financial planning, within 10 business days.

- For a list of CPAs who are also PFSs, contact the AICPA at 888-999-9256, *www.cpapfs.org*. Look under Where can I find a CPA/PFS.

- For fee-only and commission-based planners in your area, contact the Financial Planning Associate at 800-282-PLAN, *www.fpanet.org* (go to the consumer section).

Smart Questions To Ask a Financial Planner

Once you have found a potential planner (or planners, if you have two or three good recommendations), make an appointment to meet with him or her. Initial consultations are usually free because it gives you and the planner an opportunity to get acquainted. No planning actually takes place at this interview. Instead, a good planner will ask the reason for your visit, much like a doctor would ask, "What hurts?" If it is a specific problem that you need advice on, such as deciding whether to invest money in a mutual fund or a 529 plan, the planner may address the issue immediately. Still, his comments will be rather general until he has learned more about you and your financial goals and reviewed your financial documents such as tax forms and investment statements. (That will not happen until a second or third meeting.)

At this first meeting, the planner will ask you a number of questions about your current situation—that is your finances as well as some softer questions about your dreams and goals—to assess your needs and to make sure that he can handle your problems. Ideally, he should also explain his business methodology and the cost of his services. Your job is to listen, take notes if necessary, and ask some questions of your own. (Remember: You have not retained the services of the planner yet. The purpose of this initial interview is to see if you want to hire him or her.) Use the following questions as a guide:

- *What is your personality like?* Obviously, you cannot ask this question outright. You have to assess the answer from this conversation. Is he too pushy? Does he use lots of unintelligible planner's jargon, which, when questioned, he cannot simplify for you in a way that you understand? You must feel comfortable talking with this planner—just as you would with a trusted doctor or lawyer—because you will be talking with him about money, which is often a difficult topic for folks to discuss.

- *How long have you been in practice?* You do not want the new kid on the block. Look for someone who has a few years of experience, preferably in college planning. Also, ask about her background. What designations does she hold? (See the previous explanation of the various designations.)

- *What areas do you specialize in?* All planners cover most of the basic areas of personal finance, and college planning technically falls into the basic category. However, financial planners do specialize in certain areas such as retirement or estate planning. Obviously, if you go the specialized route, you want someone who specializes in college planning.

  If this is your first time working with a financial planner, you may feel that the planner *seems* knowledgeable about college planning. Do not sell yourself (or your kids) short, though. College planning can get rather tricky, especially as your child nears college age. It is easy to overestimate a *generalist's* level of expertise. Yes, he may be able to help you set up a savings plan and fill out your financial aid forms, but perhaps not more than you could do on your own. If you are going to pay someone for guidance, hire a professional who really knows the ins and outs of the college business. Most of the college planning experts interviewed for this book had their fingers on the university pulse. Because they met regularly with financial aid and admissions directors at universities, they had up-to-the-minute advice that can save parents thousands of dollars and/or get your kid into the school of his or her choice.

- *What is your fee? Do you receive commissions for the products that you sell?* If she is a fee-only planner, find out if she charges an hourly fee, a percentage of your portfolio, or an annual fee.

- *What can I expect?* After the initial consultation, some people visit a planner once or twice to solve a particular problem. Then, the people (that is you) go back to managing their own finances. Other people, however, want a long-term relationship. They want to meet regularly with a planner to discuss their progress, new goals and issues, and so on. If that is the scenario you envision, ask how frequently you can expect to meet. Every six months? Once a year? (Do not forget to ask about the price for this type of service.)

- *Who is your average client?* Many planners do the lion's share of their work with a particular type of client—self-employed workers, for instance, or folks with a net worth of $400,000 or more. You need to find a planner who frequently counsels other people like you. Otherwise, you may get inaccurate advice or below-average service. Why? A planner who handles mostly wealthy clients is more apt to spend his time with the high-rollers rather than modest-income you.

- *Whom may I call as a reference?* You will learn a lot about a prospective planner if you talk with clients (or former clients), especially those who are in financial situations similar to yours. Do not be shy about asking questions. Find out how the client's investments have performed, if the planner did what she said she would do, and what the client liked and disliked about her.

CHAPTER 6

Reducing the Tab

Most people cannot save the entire cost of a college education, but that is okay. *Really*. No one, including the colleges themselves, expects you to have four years of educational expenses parked in a money market account on the first day that your child steps foot on campus. Many parents, in fact, pay a good chunk of their child's college costs while the child is attending college. (The money comes out of their current and future income.) What is more, no one says that you must save the *entire* amount at all. Your family may qualify for a grant, a tax credit, or you may take out a low-interest-rate loan. In addition, your child may receive a scholarship and/or work part time.

What kind of assistance can you expect? The following are outlines of the types of tax credits and financial aid currently available (see Table 6.1). (In the next chapter, we will discuss how to actually apply for such aid.)

There are four basic types of aid: grants, loans, work-study jobs, and scholarships. (Because of the amount of material that needs to be covered, scholarships and loans are discussed separately in Chapters 8 and 9, respectively.) Most aid packages are a mixture of these elements. However, no matter how generous the freebie part of your financial aid package is, it probably will not cover the entire bill. Why? Grants and many scholarships are meant to fill in the gap, not give students a free ride. Most financial aid packages—even those for the neediest students—include loans and/or a work-study job.

TABLE 6.1 Federal Student Aid at a Glance

	CAMPUS-BASED AID PROGRAMS				DIRECT LOAN AND FEDERAL FAMILY EDUCATION (FEEL) PROGRAMS		
	FEDERAL PELL GRANT	FSEOG	FEDERAL WORK-STUDY	FEDERAL-PERKINS LOAN	SUBSIDIZED LOANS	UNSUBSIDIZED LOANS	PLUS LOAN
Type of Aid	Grant: Does not have to be repaid.	Grant: Does not have to be repaid.	Money is earned: Does not have to be repaid.	Loan: Must be repaid.	Loan: Must be repaid.	Loan: Must be repaid.	Loan: Must be repaid.
Other Specific Facts	Available to undergraduates only.	Not all schools participate in all campus-based programs. For undergraduates only.	Not all schools participate in all campus-based programs.	Not all schools participate in all campus-based programs.	Subsidized: Department of Education pays interest while the student is in school and during grace and deferment periods.	Unsubsidized: The borrower is responsible for interest during the life of the loan.	Available to parents of dependent undergraduate students.
Grant/Loan Limits	Up to $3,300.	Up to $4,000.	No annual maximum.	$4,000 for undergraduate students, $6,000 for graduate students.	$2,625 to $18,000, depending on grade level.	$2,625 to $18,000, depending on grade level.	Cost of attendance minus any other financial aid received.

	CAMPUS-BASED AID PROGRAMS				DIRECT LOAN AND FEDERAL FAMILY EDUCATION (FEEL) PROGRAMS		
	FEDERAL PELL GRANT	FSEOG	FEDERAL WORK-STUDY	FEDERAL-PERKINS LOAN	SUBSIDIZED LOANS	UNSUBSIDIZED LOANS	PLUS LOAN
Disbursement	School acts as the Department of Education's agent.	School disburses funds to students.	School disburses earned funds to students.	School disburses funds to students.	Direct Loans: Department of Education disburses funds directly to students. FEEL: Department of Education provides funds to schools to disburse to students.	Same as previous.	Same as previous.

Source: The U.S. Department of Education.

Grants

Grants are free gifts and are sometimes referred to as *gift aid*. You do *not* have to repay them. Unlike scholarships, however, which are also free gifts, grants are usually awarded on the basis of need only. Top-notch grades, musical talent, or a record-breaking 40-yard dash typically do not figure into the equation. When most people talk about grants, they typically mean *federal* grants offered by the U.S. government. However, many schools and some states offer grants, too.

Unfortunately, federal grants are rather limited (in terms of eligibility). Even if you do qualify, they are not all that generous. The Pell Grant, for example, is the largest federal grant program. In the 20002–2003 academic year, the Pell Grant gave students a maximum award of $4,000 per year. (You can receive only one Pell Grant per year.) The amount of money available each year varies, depending on the funding allocated to this program in the federal budget. Pell Grants are targeted toward low-income students, most of whom are from families with annual incomes below $20,000. As your family income increases, the size of your grant decreases.

If you are applying for government aid, though, this is the place to start. Applying for a Pell Grant is a prerequisite, in fact, for getting a government-subsidized student loan. (To apply, you must fill out the Free Application for Federal Student Aid [FAFSA] form. Check out Chapter 7 for the details.) For many students, Pell Grants provide a foundation of financial aid to which other aid may be added. The school must tell you in writing how much your Pell Grant award is and how and when you will be paid. Your school can apply Pell Grant funds to your school costs, pay you directly, or combine these methods.

Another type of grant is the Federal Supplemental Educational Opportunity Grant (FSEOG), which awards additional need-based money to supplement the Pell Grant. Like the Pell Grant, this money is meant for students from extremely low-income families. Pell Grant recipients with the lowest Expected Family Contributions (EFCs)(see Chapter 7 for an explanation of EFCs), in fact, will be the first to get FSEOGs. You can get between $100 and $4,000 a year, depending on when you apply, your financial need, and the funding at the school your child is attending. Unlike the federal Pell Grant, though, this grant is campus-based. That means it is administered directly by the financial aid office at each participating school; not all schools participate in this grant program.

Here is how it works: The Pell Grant program provides funds to *every* eligible student because the government guarantees that a school will get enough money so that all applicants who are eligible for Pell Grant awards will get them. With a campus-based program like an FSEOG, however, a school gets just a certain amount of money. When the money for the program is gone, no more awards can be made from that program for that year, even if there are still eligible students who have not gotten any grant money. Basically, these grants are doled out on a first-come, first-served basis. Ultimately, the amount that a student receives will depend on how early he or she applies for the money and how much FSEOG grant money the college has available. Both Pells and FSEOGs are for undergraduates only. (In some cases, a student enrolled in a post-college teacher-certification program might receive a Pell Grant.)

Loans

Over the last 20 years, loans have replaced grants as the primary source of financial aid to college students. Like federal grants, government-subsidized loans are awarded to students in need. (Unsubsidized government loans, however, are available to all students, not just those in need.) However, unlike grants, this money must be paid back. Government loans are often good sources of college financing, though, because interest rates are low and payments often do not have to be made until the student leaves college. Repayment generally begins six to nine months after graduation (or when the student leaves college). This is called a grace period. You can take up to 10 years (or longer, in some cases) to repay the loan in full. How do you apply for federal loans? You must fill out the FAFSA form. (Check out Chapter 7 for the details. You will find a sample copy of the FAFSA at the end of that chapter, too.)

Uncle Sam is not the only borrowing source in town. Several not-for-profit organizations, such as TERI and SallieMae, offer private, or *alternative,* loans at rates slightly higher than government-sponsored loans. You can also borrow money from yourself through a home-equity loan, a margin loan, or a loan against your life insurance policy or retirement savings account. (For the complete story on borrowing, see Chapter 9, which discusses the types of loans available and how to apply for them.)

Scholarships

Not all financial aid is based on need. Numerous colleges, corporations, community organizations, and churches offer full and partial scholarships. These monetary awards are based on *merit.* For students who are smart, athletic, or artistic, some scholarships can provide thousands of dollars in tuition money each year. In other cases, though, the awards are far smaller: $500 or so per year. Still, every little bit helps. Five hundred dollars may not put much of a dent in your tuition bill, but it will pay for books and some supplies. (For the lowdown on scholarships, see Chapter 8, which discusses the types of scholarships available and how to apply for them.)

Work-Study Programs

Work-study programs, such as the *Federal Work-Study* program, are different from both loans and grants. With this type of financial aid, students work at an on- or off-campus job to earn money to pay for school. If your child works on campus, he or she will usually work for the school. If the student works off campus, the employer will usually be a private, nonprofit organization or a public agency because the program encourages community service work. How much will students earn? The government subsidizes a portion of the paycheck; the college or employer pays the rest. Typically, the student works on an hourly basis and earns at least the minimum wage. Your child may earn a bit more, too. Because the job must be relevant to your child's course of study, a Federal Work-Study job can sometimes help your child gain valuable work experience while he or she is still in school.

State Aid

States also offer financial aid—in the form of grants, loans, and scholarships—to their residents. To qualify, you *and* your child must be residents. In some states, you can still qualify for aid, even if your child attends a public or private college in another state. In Connecticut, for example, residents can qualify for state aid no matter what school they attend. In Maryland, you can only get state money for an out-of-state school if your child is pursing a unique course study. That is, no other school in Maryland offers a comparable program.

To find out what is available, contact the state higher education agency in your home state. (The phone numbers are listed at the end of this chapter.) These agencies can give you information about state aid, including aid from the Leveraging Educational Assistance Partnership (LEAP) program, which is funded jointly by individual states and the U.S. Department of Education. In addition, these agencies can give you information about the Robert C. Byrd Honors Scholarship Program (Byrd Program). To qualify for aid under this program, your child must demonstrate outstanding academic achievement and show promise of continued academic excellence.

Institutional Aid

Each university and college offers its own aid packages, too, in the form of grants, loans, and scholarships. These awards are based on need or merit and vary from one institution to another. Unlike aid offered by the federal government, though, which is awarded based on the *federal methodology* (see Chapter 7), this aid is often calculated based on the *institutional methodology*. Each individual college or university decides on what basis it will disburse funds to new students. This money is awarded on a first-come, first-served basis. Each school typically has a certain amount to spend on financial assistance to students. Once that allotment is gone, the school has no more to give, even if it wanted to.

Sources of Funds for College

Savings and investments. Obviously, the sooner you start saving, the better.

Your current income. You will probably have to dig into your own pockets as your child is attending school. Chances are, though, you may have more discretionary income now that your kids are older.

Student jobs. Your kids can work during vacations and/or part time when school is in session. Work-study programs let students earn some of their tuition by working at a job on or near campus.

Grants. Free money that is given to students based on need. Unfortunately, most middle-class parents do not qualify.

Scholarships. More free money that is not necessarily need-based. Many schools offer awards to students who are gifted in academics, athletics, or the arts.

Loans. Student and personal loans are a common way to secure the needed funds. Obviously, this is the most costly source. Young college graduates just starting out will be saddled with loan repayments for years; otherwise, you will have to assume the debt just when you are probably thinking about retirement.

Tax Breaks

There are tax breaks for *saving* for college, through Coverdell education savings accounts or qualified tuition plans. But there are also several tax breaks for paying for college, including deductions and credits. You may qualify for an above-the-line deduction (whether or not you itemize your other deductions). Even better, you may be able to take a tax credit for certain higher education costs.

College Tax Credits and Deductions

What is the difference between a tax *deduction* and a tax *credit*? A tax credit is more valuable than a tax deduction, says Brian E. Glickman, a certified public accountant who runs Tuition Solutions, a college planning firm in Smithtown, New York. Here is why: A tax deduction reduces your taxable income. A $1,000 tax deduction, for example, would save you $270 in taxes (if you were in the 27 percent tax bracket). A tax credit reduces the amount of income tax you pay, dollar for dollar. A $1,000 tax credit, in any tax bracket, would save you $1,000 in taxes. A credit therefore saves you more than a deduction. Here is how they stack up against each other:

$1,000 tax deduction #	versus.	$1,000 tax credit ##
Reduces taxable income	*	Reduces actual amount of tax
Paid		
Tax savings = $270	*	Tax savings = $1,000

#Assumes a 27% tax bracket
##Applicable in any tax bracket

During the first two years of college or vocational school, the Hope Scholarship Credit lets parents take a tax credit of up to $1,500 each year for each student in the family. Students must be enrolled at least half-time to qualify, and the credit is taken against qualified expenses. Basically, that is tuition and required fees. Room and board, books and supplies, and transportation do not count in this tabulation.

Here is how it works: The amount of the credit equals 100 percent of the first $1,000 of those qualified expenses, plus 50 percent of the second $1,000, for a maximum amount of $1,500. (The amount of expenses are adjusted for inflation after 2002, but due to low inflation there is no adjustment in this amount for 2003). Now, why is this advantageous? A tax credit is better than a tax deduction because a credit is subtracted directly from your federal income tax, dollar for dollar. A deduction, however, is subtracted from your income before you calculate your tax and yields much less than dollar-for-dollar savings. Ultimately, this tax credit puts an extra $1,500 into your pocket, instead of Uncle Sam's, each year.

You are eligible for the full tax credit if you are a married couple filing jointly and earn up to $82,000 annually in adjusted gross income in 2002 ($83,000 in 2003). Single filers can earn up to $41,000. The credit is gradually reduced for higher-income families. If your family earns more than double your limit, you do not qualify for any credit at all. But if your income is too high to permit you to claim the credit, you can opt to let your child claim it (assuming he or she has taxable income and can benefit from it), even though you paid the expenses. All you must do is *not* claim a dependency exemption for your child.

During your child's junior and senior years of college, the Lifetime Learning Credit kicks in. This credit is worth 20 percent annually of the first $5,000 you spend on those qualified expenses (for a maximum of $1,000), through the year 2002; after 2002, the credit jumps to 20 percent of the first $10,000 in expenses (for a maximum of $2,000). This credit has the same income restrictions as the Hope Scholarship.

Unlike the Hope Scholarship, however, the Lifetime Learning Credit is not adjusted for inflation. More importantly, the Lifetime Learning Credit is claimed per family, not per child. That means, even though you may have two or three kids in college during the same year, you only get *one* Lifetime Learning Credit per year. (With a Hope Scholarship Credit, remember, you get as many credits as you have students in college.) You can, however, take a Lifetime Learning Credit and one or more Hope Scholarships in the same year. Obviously, the credits cannot apply to the same student.

Finally, there is another, newer option, which came about with the Economic Growth and Tax Relief Reconciliation Act of 2001. Instead of taking either the Hope Tax Credit or the Lifetime Learning Tax Credit, taxpayers can take an above-the-line *deduction* for qualified higher education expenses. (This will mostly benefit parents who make too much money to qualify for either of those tax credits.) In 2002 and 2003, married couples with adjusted gross incomes up to $130,000 will be entitled to a deduction of $3,000 per year. (To qualify, single taxpayers can have an adjusted gross income up to $65,000.) In 2004 and 2005, the deduction will increase to $4,000 (with the same income limits just described). However, higher income families, that is, single taxpayers with adjusted incomes up to $80,000 and joint filers with adjusted incomes up to $160,000, can take a maximum deduction of $2,000 in 2004 and 2005. After 2005, alas, you are out of luck. Uncle Sam is only offering this deduction for four years!

HOPE SCHOLARSHIP CREDIT

- Up to $1,500 credit per student.
- Available only for the first two years of college and only for two years per eligible student.
- Student must be enrolled at least half-time.

LIFETIME LEARNING CREDIT

- Up to $1,000 credit per family; after 2002, it is up to $2,000 per family.
- Available for any post-secondary education and for an unlimited number of years.
- Student does not need to be pursuing a degree; a student qualifies if taking one or more courses.

COLLEGE TUITION DEDUCTION

- Ranges from a $2,000 to $4,000 deduction per year.
- Available for any year of college.
- Deduction is only available for four years: 2002 to 2005.

To maximize your tax savings, you will need to plan ahead. If you qualify for the Hope Scholarship Credit, the Lifetime Learning Credit, *and* the College Tuition Deduction, you will have to figure out which tax strategy saves you more. (Your tax preparer or financial planner can help you figure this out.) The College Tax Deduction is only available for the next four years, however. So, unless your child is going to attend college soon, you may not have to make any decision: The only choice may be the tax credits. Surprisingly, most people who qualify for these credits can save more than they think. Why? Students typically attend college for five—and not four—*tax* years, thus entitling you to an extra credit. (See the explanation at the end of this example.) If you qualify for the Hope Scholarship Credit and the Lifetime Learning Credit and if you have just one child in college, here is what your tax credit schedule might look like:

2002	Freshman year (fall):	$1,500 Hope Scholarship
2003	Freshman year (spring) and sophomore year (fall):	$1,500 Hope Scholarship
2004	Sophomore year (spring) and junior year (fall):	$2,000 Lifetime Learning Credit
2005	Junior year (spring) and senior year (fall):	$2,000 Lifetime Learning Credit
2006	Senior year (spring):	$2,000 Lifetime Learning Credit
	Total TAX CREDITS	$9,000

Note: Even if your child attends college for the customary four years, for tax purposes, he or she is really in school for five years. Most students, remember, attend college for four years: freshman, sophomore, junior, and senior years. Those four years are generally then divided into two semesters: spring and fall. Here is the catch: The school year is not the same as the tax year. Freshman year, for instance, starts in the fall of 2002, let us say, but the spring semester, that is the second half of freshman year, takes place in 2003, which is a different tax year. The same thing happens in sophomore year, junior year, and senior year, so that by the time your son or daughter graduates, his or her college career will likely span four college years but five different calendar or tax years.

If you have more than one child in college at the same time, however, you may be able to claim both tax credits in the same year. (Unfortunately, as you will see in the following, you will not be able to do this every year.) Let us assume that you have two children: Holly is 18 and Ryan is 16. Here is how your tax credit schedule might play out:

2002	Holly's freshman year (fall)	$1,500 Hope Scholarship
2003	Holly's freshman year (spring) and sophomore year (fall)	$1,500 Hope Scholarship
2004	Holly's sophomore year (spring) and junior year (fall)	$2,000 Lifetime Learning Credit
	Ryan's freshman year (fall)	$1,500 Hope Scholarship

2005	Holly's junior year (spring) and senior year (fall)	$2,000 Lifetime Learning Credit
	Ryan's freshman year (spring) and sophomore year (fall)	$1,500 Hope Scholarship
2006	Holly's senior year (spring) Ryan's sophomore year (spring) and junior year (fall)	$2,000 Lifetime Learning Credit (Ryan would normally qualify for a $2,000 Lifetime Learning Credit at this point, but his sister has already taken one. You cannot take more than one Lifetime Learning Credit per year, per household.)
2007	Ryan's junior year (spring) and senior year (fall)	$2,000 Lifetime Learning Credit
2008	Ryan's senior year (spring)	$2,000 Lifetime Learning Credit
	Total Tax Credits	$16,000

FYI

For more information on these credits, read IRS Publication 970, Tax Benefits for Higher Education (to order, call 1-800-829-3676, or download at *www.irs.gov*)

Smart Ways To Save

In addition to Uncle Sam's generosity, you can shave even more money off that college tab, if you know where to look:

Consider a school near home. That could save you a bundle. If your child can live at home and commute to campus, you will save on room and board expenses.

Consider a two-year community college for the first two years. Even if your child is planning on earning a four-year degree, she might want to think about attending a community college for the first two years. Why? Community colleges are partially funded by local and state taxes, so they are usually less expensive than most four-year schools. (If she continues to live at home while attending, your daughter will save you additional cash on room and board.) After two years, she can transfer to the four-year school and complete her education there. Of course, you will need to make sure ahead of time that the courses your daughter takes at the community college will transfer to the four-year school that she wants to attend, and that they will count toward her bachelor's degree.

Attend college part-time. Your child will be able to work (and thus fund some of her own college tuition) if she only goes to school part-time. Part-time students often pay less, too. The downside? It will take longer for your child to complete her education if she attends school part-time rather than full-time.

If you are eligible for financial aid, part-time students usually get less aid than full-time students, and the college experience is different when you are a part-timer. Many would say it is less fun and more like work. Some part-time students lose interest (and thus drop out) because it is hard to stay focused for that length of time. (It could take eight or more years to graduate!)

Attend an in-state school. Public universities generally charge out-of-state residents a higher tuition to attend. If you live in New Jersey, for example, you will pay more to attend the State University at Binghamton, New York, than students who live in New York State.

Get Grandma or Grandpa to chip in. Grandparents often want to help out with college tuition. If they are financially well off, they may also be concerned about reducing the size of their estates. Often, they can accomplish both goals by gifting money to young William, III, but it is not as simple as writing a check. The money must be given according to certain rules. Because this can be a rather complicated business, I need more than a paragraph to discuss the matter successfully. See the section called "Getting Grandparents To Help."

Get a head start in high school. When they are juniors and seniors in high school, encourage your kids to take Advanced Placement (AP) courses in biology, trigonometry, and various other subjects. Many colleges give credit for these courses. That means if your son takes enough high school AP courses, he may be able to cut out a semester or two of course work at the university. That will cut your four-year bill by up to one-fourth.

Students can also accelerate their college studies through credit-by-examination programs, such as the College-Level Examination Program (CLEP), which is sponsored by the college board. Essentially, students earn credits by simply taking an exam rather than attending a class. CLEP currently offers general exams that cover course material usually required in the first two years of college as well as numerous subject exams. (Obviously, this study route requires a high degree of student motivation.)

Check with your employer. Some employers offer education assistance to employees' kids. Employers can kick in some cash to help workers pay their child's college tuition bills. As long as the employer's gift does not exceed $5,250 per year, the money is not reported as income on his or her W-2 form.

Get a job at the college. Students whose parents work at the college itself can often attend that school for free. (We are talking tuition here; generally, you must still pay for room and board.) To take advantage of this freebie, you (the parent) do not necessarily have to be a professor. You could do administrative work, for instance. In some cases, your child may not even have to attend that particular school to take advantage of this free tuition. Some schools have reciprocity with other colleges. If you work at one college, your child may be able to attend those reciprocity schools for free, too. The only catch with this deal? The cost of the tuition (if you had to pay it, like most other parents) may be added to your annual salary as *income*. You will owe income tax on this additional amount.

Attend college as an independent student. When you apply for student aid, it will make a difference if your child is dependent upon you, his parents, or is independent and living on his or her own. Independent students generally qualify for more aid because they tend to have lower incomes and fewer assets than their adult parents. Is your child independent? This is not a trick question, but the answer is not as obvious as it may appear. An independent status is not granted just because the child appears to be living on his or her own. (You could easily still be supporting him or her.) Rather, the child must meet one of the following criteria to be classified as an independent student:

- Parents are deceased
- Age 24 or older
- Married
- Veteran of the U.S. armed forces
- Has legal dependents (other than a spouse)
- Enrolled in a graduate or professional educational program (beyond a bachelor's degree)

Join the military. For students who are willing to do time in the armed forces, the following suggestions can help reduce tuition costs:

- *Attend a military academy.* These four-year colleges offer free education to students who pass their rigorous admissions process and commit to serve after graduation.
- *Enroll in the Reserve Officer Training Corps (ROTC) Program.* ROTC will bankroll little Debbie's tuition (plus fees and books) and give her a monthly allowance. Again, she must commit to a number of years of active duty after college. Contact your local U.S. Army, Navy, Air Force, or Marines recruiting center for more information.
- *Join the armed forces before going to college.* Your child can then take advantage of the Montgomery GI Bill, which provides financial support to those who attend school after serving in the military. In addition, students can also earn college credit for some military training.
- *Join the armed forces after going to college.* The U.S. Army can help repay some of your college debt if your child is willing to sign up after graduation. Through its Loan Repayment Program, the U.S. Army will repay up to $65,000 on specific federally guaranteed loans. New recruits must enlist for three years.

Volunteer. Students (or graduates) who volunteer for an AmeriCorps program earn education awards in return for national service. Full-time volunteers log about 1,700 hours and earn an award of $4,725. Part-timers log some 900 hours and earn an award of $2,362.50. Some full-time volunteers are also eligible for a modest monthly living allowance of $400 to $700. However, the education awards must be used to pay for college or to pay back student loans. Also, both the awards and the monthly living allowances are considered to be taxable income. For more information, contact the Corporation for National Service: 1-800-942-2677, *www.cns.gov*.

Work part-time. Most students work-for-pay while attending college to help defray some of the cost of their education. Some parents and educators question the soundness of this strategy. Isn't college the student's full-time job? Isn't the student sacrificing valuable study time (and thus hindering his academic performance) by working for a few extra bucks an hour? Maybe, but he is also gaining some on-the-job experience (that is, learning to deal courteously with customers or running a cash register) as well as meeting new people, learning about juggling responsibilities and, yes, earning a few bucks.

Obviously, each student must make this decision for himself. Is the time spent at a job worth the time spent away from one's studies? A recent study, however, found that students who worked up to 20 hours per week were no less likely to finish their bachelor's degree than students who did not work at all. However, those who worked more than 20 hours were less likely to finish their degree within five years. According to the National Center for Education Statistics, most four-year college students who work do work less than 20 hours per week. Unfortunately, the study does not say anything about how the grades of the working students compared to the nonworking students (see the following minitable).

HOURS TYPICALLY WORKED PER WEEK WHILE ENROLLED FULL-TIME IN COLLEGE

Hours Worked	Public four-year (in-state)	Public two-year (in-state)	Private four-year
None	26%	17%	28%
1 to 10	12%	6%	10%
11 to 20	34%	29%	33%
21 to 39	21%	35%	26%
40 or more	6%	13%	8%

Source: U.S. Department of Education, National Center for Education Statistics, and National Postsecondary Student Aid Study.

Getting Grandparents To Help

Has Grandma hinted on several occasions that she has got money set aside for Junior's college education? Before you broach the subject—tactfully, of course, because you do not want to appear too calculating—you should understand the ways in which people can gift money and how such gifts affect their estates and your child's chances of financial aid.

In most cases, grandparents either give the money directly to the grandchild or they set up a custodial account, such as a Uniform Gifts to Minors Act (UGMA), in the child's name. As discussed in Chapter 3, the trouble with setting up the custodial account is that the school will expect a greater percentage of the student's money (in this case, the custodial account set up by Grandma) to be used to pay for college tuition than assets held in the parent's name. (Assets held in the grandmother's name would not be counted at all.) Therefore, unless you know for sure that your child will not qualify for financial aid, do not set up a custodial account. There are other ways to get the money from Grandma to grandson.

One strategy is to let Grandma wait until college begins, but *after* the financial aid award has been granted for the year, to give some money to the student. This is a great way for grandparents to funnel smaller amounts of money to grandkids—without affecting a student's chances for financial aid, says Raymond D. Loewe, a chartered financial consultant and the president of College Money, a college financial planning firm in Marlton, New Jersey.

That is not all. Although financial aid may be the hot topic on your mind, Grandma may be worried about the taxes due on these gifts and other ways, in general, to reduce the size of her taxable estate. These are common estate planning issues that concern taxpayers, especially older taxpayers like Grandma. (The Economic Growth and Tax Relief Reconciliation Act of 2001 supposedly repeals the estate tax. However, what the actual result of this tax cut will be is debatable. Under this new tax act, the estate tax would not be repealed until the year 2010, but it may only be for that one year. Because of budget constraints, it is possible that the estate tax could be reinstated in 2011. So do not count on those estate tax savings yet!) What can Grandma do then? She can give her grandson up to $11,000 per year without incurring any gift tax (the limit may be higher after 2003). Of course, this annual gift tax *exclusion* does not apply to just Grandma and her grandson. Anyone can give up to $11000, per year, to as many people as you want, without incurring that gift tax. If you are married, you and your spouse can give (as a couple) up to $22,000 per person, per year, without any gift tax liability.

Perhaps Grandma is not happy with this vague sort of gifting arrangement. Maybe she wants a more systematic plan. Loewe has a suggestion, which works great, he says, for the grandparent who wants to help, but cannot commit a large sum of money. Here is Loewe's plan:

Many grandparents have CDs that have been put away for emergencies. They reinvest the income on those CDs and continue to roll them over on their maturity dates. Instead of doing that, however, the grandparents could deposit that CD money into a tax-free bond unit trust. The grandparent would retain complete control over the funds and could redeem the fund at any time. (This is not a custodial account.) Interest from the account, which is tax free, could then be gifted to the student monthly, quarterly, or whenever the grandparents felt like it. The grandparents could stop payments to the student at any time, and they could then use the money for themselves or another student. Set up correctly, this plan is tax free and will not hurt the student's ability to obtain financial aid.

What if Grandma wants to give a more substantial amount of money? She has several options. First, in addition to the $11,000 exclusion, there is also what is called an *unlimited gift tax exclusion*. Grandma (or anyone else, for that matter, who wants to help you out financially) can give your son an unlimited amount of money to pay for college, and she will not have to pay tax on it. To take advantage of this exclusion, however, Grandma must pay the money *directly* to the college. Writing a check directly to her grandson, even if the young man uses the funds immediately to pay tuition bills, will void this exclusion. In addition, Grandma may only pay for tuition. Other college-related expenses, such as room and board and books, do not qualify for the unlimited exclusion. These other expenses do qualify for the $11,000 exclusion, however. (For your information, this unlimited gift tax exclusion also applies to medical expenses.) From a financial aid standpoint, though, direct payments such as these are treated as a *scholarship* by the college, says Loewe. That means your child's need-based financial aid eligibility will be reduced, dollar for dollar, as a result of Grandma's generosity.

Grandma could also gift money to a 529 savings plan (discussed in detail in Chapter 5) on her grandson's behalf. She could gift $11,000 per year (and not owe any federal gift tax), or she could gift a $55,000 lump sum (and again, not owe any federal gift tax). There is a special gift tax rule that lets you make a $55,000 lump-sum contribution rather than five of the $11,000 annual tax-free gifts. How will this affect the student's chances of financial aid? Most 529 plans are set up so that the assets belong to the custodian. If the custodian is not the parent or the student, then the asset does not come into the financial aid calculation. Even if the parents set up the 529 plan (and thus act as custodian) and Grandma just contributes that $11,000 every year or a lump sum, the assets would still belong to the parent and not the student. You would not, then, have that custodial account problem of being asked to pay a greater percentage of the funds because it is the student's money. Or so you would think. Unfortunately, the money withdrawn from a 529 plan is considered income to the student. Under federal guidelines, the student is expected to contribute 50 percent of his income (above a minimum level) to pay those college bills. That means you are losing 50 cents on every dollar of aid received, says Loewe. A $10,000 withdrawal from a 529 plan, for example, would reduce your financial aid by $5,000. The prepaid plans are even worse. With these plans, says Loewe, withdrawals reduce need-based financial aid *dollar for dollar.*

Gifting directly to the student, though, is the smartest course (from an estate planning perspective), if Grandma wants to give her grandson money for college by selling an appreciated asset such as stocks. If Grandma cashes out the stocks herself and then gives her grandson or the school the money directly, she will pay a capital gains tax of 20 percent on the sale of the stocks. Depending on how much those stocks have appreciated over time, the capital gains tax due could be substantial. However, if Grandma gifts the stocks to her grandson and lets *him* then sell the shares to raise cash for college, he would pay the capital gains on the stocks. That gain would then be taxed at his tax rate, which could be as low as 8 percent, or less than half what Grandma paid. (Again, this capital gains savings is not limited to grandmas. Parents can give appreciated stocks to their own children to save on taxes. However, once you give the stocks to the child, the money garnered from the sale is the child's to use as he sees fit.)

Another option for Grandma is to set up an Educational Needs Trust. Under this arrangement, Grandma would take the money out of her estate and make an irrevocable gift (that means she cannot take the money back) to her grandson. (Grandma could set this trust up for more than one grandchild.) This is a formal trust, however, so the amount of the gift, says Loewe, must be fairly large to offset the cost of the trust. Here is how it works, says Loewe: The trust invests its principal in loans to the grandchildren during college. Those loans are repaid after college. The principal is distributed to the grandchildren after all trust beneficiaries have repaid their loans. Any taxes on investment income are paid by the trust. This type of trust should not hurt the student's ability to receive financial aid.

State Agencies

Alabama
Alabama Commission on Higher
  Education
P.O. Box 302000
Montgomery, AL 36130-2000
334-242-2274 / 800-843-8534
www.ache.state.al.us

Alaska
Alaska Commission on Postsecondary
  Education
3030 Vintage Boulevard
Juneau, AK 99801-7100
907-465-6741 / 800-441-2962
http://www.state.ak.us/acpel

Arizona
Arizona Commission for Postsecondary
  Education
2020 North Central Avenue, Suite 550
Phoenix, AZ 85004-4503
602-258-2435
www.acpe.asu.edu

Arkansas
Arkansas Department of Higher
  Education
114 East Capitol
Little Rock, AR 72201-3818
501-371-2000
www.arkansashighered.com

California
California Student Aid Commission
P.O. Box 419027
Rancho Cordova, CA 95741-9027
916-526-7590 / 888-221-7268
www.csac.ca.gov

Colorado
Colorado Commission on Higher
    Education
13800 Lawrence Street, Suite 1200
Denver, CO 80204
303-866-2723
www.state.co.us/cche_dir/hecche.html

Connecticut
Connecticut Department of Higher
    Education
61 Woodland Street
Hartford, CT 06105-2326
860-947-1855 / 800-842-0229
www.ctdhe.org

Delaware
Delaware Higher Education Commission
820 North French Street, 5th Floor
Wilmington, DE 19801
302-577-3240 / 800-292-7935
www.doe.state.de.us/high-ed

District of Columbia
Office of Postsecondary Education
    Research and Assistance
2100 Martin Luther King Jr. Avenue, S.E.,
    Suite 401
Washington, DC 20020
202-698-2400

Florida
Office of Student Financial Assistance
1940 North Monroe Street, Suite 70
Tallahassee, FL 32303-4759
850-410-5200 / 800-366-347
www.floridastudentfinancialaid.org

Georgia
Georgia Student Finance Authority
2082 East Exchange Place, Suite 230

Tucker, GA 30084
770-724-9000 / 800-776-6878
www.gsfc.org/main/main.cfm

Hawaii
Hawaii State Postsecondary Education
    Commission
2444 Dole Street, Room 209
Honolulu, HI 96822-2302
808-956-8213
www.hern.hawaii.edu/hern

Idaho
Idaho State Board of Education
P.O. Box 83720
Boise, ID 83720-0027
208-334-2270
www.idahoboardofed.org

Illinois
Illinois Student Assistance Commission
1755 Lake Cook Road
Deerfield, IL 60015-5209
847-948-8500 / 800-899-4722
www.isac-online.org/gateway.html

Indiana
State Student Assistance Commission of
    Indiana
150 West Market Street, Suite 500
Indianapolis, IN 46204-2811
317-232-2350 / 888-528-4719
www.in.gov/ssaci

Iowa
Iowa College Student Aid Commission
200 Tenth Street, 4th Floor
Des Moines, IA 50309
515-242-3344 / 800-383-4222
www.state.ia.us/collegeaid

Kansas
Kansas Board of Regents
1000 SW Jackson Street, Suite 520
Topeka, KS 66602-1368
785-296-3421
www.kansasregents.org

Kentucky
Kentucky Higher Education Assistance
  Authority
1050 U.S. 127 South
Frankfort, KY 40601-4323
800-928-8926
www.kheaa.com

Louisiana
Louisiana Student Financial Assistance
  Commission
P.O. Box 91202
Baton Rouge, LA 70821-9202
225-922-1012 / 800-259-5626
www.osfa.state.la.us

Maine
Maine Education Assistance Division
5 Community Drive
Augusta, ME 04332-0949
207-623-3263 / 800-228-3734
www.famemaine.com

Maryland
Maryland Higher Education Commission
16 Francis Street
Annapolis, MD 21401-1781
410-260-4565 / 800-735-2258
www.mhec.state.md.us

Massachusetts
Massachusetts Board of Higher
  Education
One Ashburton Place, Room 1401
Boston, MA 02108
617-994-6950
www.mass.edu

Michigan
Michigan Higher Education Assistance
  Authority
Office of Scholarships and Grants
P.O. Box 30462
Lansing, MI 48909-7962
517-373-3394 / 888-447-2687
www.michigan.gov/mistudentaid

Minnesota
Minnesota Higher Education Services
  Office
1450 Energy Park Drive, Suite 350
St. Paul, MN 55108-5227
651-642-0533 / 800-657-3866
www.mheso.state.mn.us

Mississippi
Mississippi Office of Student Financial
  Aid
3825 Ridgewood Road
Jackson, MS 39211-6453
601-432-6997 / 800-327-2980
www.ihl.state.ms.us

Missouri
Missouri Department of Higher
  Education
3515 Amazonas Drive
Jefferson City, MO 65109-5717
573-751-2361 / 800-473-6757
www.cbhe.state.mo.us

Montana
Montana University System
P.O. Box 203101
Helena, MT 59620-3103
406-444-6570
www.montana.edu/wwwoche

Nebraska
Nebraska Coordinating Commission for
  Postsecondary Education
P.O. Box 95005
Lincoln, NE 68509-5005
402-471-2847
*www.ccpe.state.ne.us/Publicdoc/CCPE/D
  efault.asp*

Nevada
Nevada Department of Education
700 East 5th Street
Carson City, NV 89701
775-687-9200
www.nde.state.nv.us

New Hampshire
New Hampshire Postsecondary
  Education Commission
3 Barrell Court, Suite 300
Concord, NH 03301-8543
603-271-2555
www.state.nh.us/postsecondary

New Jersey
Higher Education Student Assistance
  Authority
P.O. Box 540
Trenton, NJ 08625-0540
609-588-3226 / 800-792-8670
www.hesaa.org

New Mexico
New Mexico Commission on Higher
  Education
1068 Cerrillos Road
Santa Fe, NM 87505
505-827-7383 / 800-279-9777
www.nmche.org

New York
New York State Higher Education
  Services Corporation
99 Washington Avenue
Albany, NY 12255
518-473-1574 / 888-697-4372
www.hesc.com

North Carolina
North Carolina State Education
  Assistance Authority
P.O. Box 13663
Research Triangle Park, NC 27709-3663
919-549-8614 / 800-700-1775
www.ncseaa.edu

North Dakota
North Dakota University System
600 East Boulevard Avenue
Bismarck, NJ 58505-0230
701-328-4114
www.ndus.edu

Ohio
Ohio Board of Regents
P.O. Box 182452

Columbus, OH 43218-2452
614-466-7420 / 888-833-1133
www.regents.state.oh.us/sgs

Oklahoma
Oklahoma State Regents for Higher
  Education
655 Research Parkway, Suite 200
Oklahoma City, OK 73104
405-225-9100 / 800-858-1840
www.okhighered.org

Oregon
Oregon Student Assistance Commission
1500 Valley River Drive, Suite 100
Eugene, OR 97401
541-687-7400 / 800-452-8807
www.ossc.state.or.us

Pennsylvania
Office of Postsecondary and Higher
  Education
333 Market Street
Harrisburg, PA 17126
717-787-5041
*www.paehighered.state.pa.us/higher/site
  /default.asp*

Rhode Island
Rhode Island Higher Education
  Assistance Authority
560 Jefferson Boulevard
Warwick, RI 02886
401-736-1100 / 800-922-9855
www.riheaa.org

South Carolina
South Carolina Commission on Higher
  Education
1333 Main Street, Suite 200
Columbia, SC 29201
803-737-2260 / 877-349-7183
www.che400.state.sc.us

South Dakota
South Dakota Board of Regents
306 East Capitol Avenue, Suite 200
Pierre, SD 57501
605-773-3455
www.ris.sdbor.edu

Tennessee
Tennessee Higher Education Commission
Parkway Towers, Suite 1950
404 James Robertson Parkway
Nashville, TN 37243-0830
615-741-3605
www.state.tn.us/thec

Texas
Texas Higher Education Coordinating
    Board
P.O. Box 12788
Austin, TX 78711
512-427-6101 / 800-242-3062
www.thecb.state.tx.us/ctc

Utah
Utah State Board of Regents
60 South 400 West
Salt Lake City, UT 84101
801-321-7100
www.utahsbr.edu

Vermont
Vermont Student Assistance Corporation
P.O. Box 2000
Winooski, VT 05404-2601
802-655-9602 / 800-642-3177
www.vsac.org

Virginia
Virginia State Council of Higher
    Education
101 North 14th Street, 9th Floor
Richmond, VA 23219
804-225-2600
www.schev.edu

Washington
Washington State Higher Education
    Coordinating Board
917 Lakeridge Way
P.O. Box 43430
Olympia, WA 98504-3430
360-753-7800
www.hecb.wa.gov

West Virginia
West Virginia Higher Education Policy
    Commission
1018 Kanawha Boulevard, East
Charleston, WV 25301
304-558-2101
www.hepc.wvnet.edu

Wisconsin
Wisconsin Higher Educational Aids
    Board
131 West Wilsm Street, Room 902
Madison, WI 53707
608-267-2206
http://heab.state.wi.us

Wyoming
Wyoming Student Financial Aid
174 Knight Hall
Laramie, WY 82071-3335
307-766-2116
www.uwyo.edu

CHAPTER 7

Applying for Financial Aid

Know what the most common mistake that parents make about college is? Misjudging how much financial aid they can expect. Some families never even bother applying for aid because they automatically assume they will not get any. We make too much money. Oh, really? Although income does play a major role in determining aid, it is not the only factor. There are several situations, such as having two or more kids attending college at the same time, which may qualify you for federal financial aid despite your robust family income. To qualify for some institutional aid offered from the colleges themselves, you often have to be rejected for federal aid first.

In addition, institutional financial aid packages vary significantly from school to school. The amount of aid that your family will get is determined by your financial situation, yes, but it also depends on what the particular school has to offer. Some schools may offer a more attractive financial aid package because they really want your child to attend their school and/or they have deeper financial aid pockets to draw from. What is more, if your family does not qualify for need-based aid, you may qualify for merit aid.

The moral of this story, then? Even if you do not think you qualify, you should apply for financial aid every year. You have nothing to lose (and obviously everything to gain). A small change in your family's circumstances might make you eligible one year even though you were denied aid for the previous year.

The Different Types of Financial Aid

All financial aid is not created equal. Some aid is, as many parents imagine it, free. These are grants and scholarships discussed in Chapters 6 and 8, respectively. Other aid is not free. Some portion of your child's financial aid package may be loans that have to be paid back. (Loans are discussed in detail in Chapter 9.) In general, there are two basic types of financial aid:

- *Need-based financial aid.* All this means is that you cannot afford to pay your child's tuition-based on your family's income and assets. (The actual amount that the government and the colleges expect you to pay, based on your income and assets, is called your Expected Family Contribution [EFC]. Need-based aid is still the most widely used type of aid, says Raymond D. Loewe, a chartered financial consultant and the president of College Money, a college financial planning firm in Marlton, New Jersey. Basically, the college must develop a financial aid package to make up the difference between the cost of college and what the student's parents can afford to pay, if the college wants a particular student to attend its school.

- *Merit-based financial aid. Th*is type of aid is not based on your finances, but on what your kid can do (such as playing the piano or sprinting down the track), or, in some cases, who your kid is (such as a Native American or a blood relation of one of our country's founding fathers). Most merit-based aid, says Loewe, comes in the form of scholarships or grants. (Need-based aid, by contrast, might be offered in the form of loans and work-study jobs as well as scholarships and grants.) Schools generally offer three types of merit aid: athletic scholarships for students who will play a certain sport on behalf of the college, academic scholarships for top students, and talent scholarships for students who exhibit exceptional musical, artistic, or dramatic talents.

Are You Eligible for Aid?

The amount of financial aid that you qualify for is determined by something called *financial need.* The federal government uses a specific formula, known as the *federal methodology*, to calculate each family's financial need, which then determines their eligibility for federal and state financial aid (as well as institutional aid at some colleges). Private universities generally use a different need-analysis formula called the *institutional methodology.*

Here is how these formulas work, roughly: First, you fill out the Free Application for Federal Student Aid (FAFSA) form. This form (discussed in more detail in the "Understanding the Financial Aid Forms" section) is used by all public universities. Private schools will use this form, too, for doling out federal financial aid. However, they often use the Profile (see the "Understanding the

Financial Aid Forms" section), another form that asks for additional information to determine eligibility for their own institutional aid.

The FAFSA asks you to include information about your family's income, assets, household size, the number of kids you have in college at the same time, and several other factors. All of this information is then processed to give you your EFC. Basically, this is the amount of money, based on your income, assets, and other factors, that the government says you can afford to pay for your child's college education. The EFC, then, is the amount you are expected to cough up for college.

What about those stratospheric numbers discussed in Chapter 1? If your family is expected to pay just your EFC, then who pays the remainder of that college bill? Good question. Let us go to the next step. The cost of your child's education is assessed by the college that your child wants to attend. The college bill includes tuition, room and board, and other expenses, such as books and supplies. Your EFC is then subtracted from this cost. The amount that remains is your family's financial need. This financial need is what financial aid *should* cover. (However, as you will see in the following, the system does not work perfectly. Financial aid simply cannot cover 100 percent of every needy family's costs.)

Let us look at that EFC a bit closer. Basically, it is a measurement of what you, the student's parents, can afford to pay for college. It is not the actual sticker price that is quoted in the news (and which was discussed in Chapter 1.) In fact, whether you attend a public college that charges $8,000 per year or an elite private school that charges $30,000 per year, your EFC could actually be the same (or nearly the same).

Your EFC varies not by the school per se, but by the formula used to determine the EFC. As mentioned earlier, there are two main formulas currently used: the federal methodology (used by the government and public colleges), which uses the FAFSA form, and the institutional methodology (used by many private colleges), which uses the Profile form. When public or private schools dole out federal aid, they must use the federal methodology. However, when handing out their own institutional aid, private schools may use a different method (generally, the institutional methodology, calculated on the Profile form).

FINANCIAL AID FORMULA

Your EFC is used in the following equation to determine your financial need:

Cost of attendance
$$\frac{- \text{ EFC}}{\text{Financial need}}$$

In general, families of modest means should have a lower EFC than wealthier families. (In other words, they will pay less.) However, that does not mean that all families who fall within a certain income category will necessarily have similar EFCs. Despite similar incomes, one family's ability to pay can vary considerably from another family's because your EFC is not based solely on your income (see sidebar).

However, how much you will actually wind up paying for college may be quite different than your EFC. Why? Aid policies differ from one school to another. Every school does not offer the same amount and type of aid, and not every university has enough money available to meet the full financial needs of every applicant. Some colleges, for example, cannot pay 100 percent of any applicant's needs. Other schools can meet some applicants' financial needs (the school may pay 100 percent of a gifted musician's need, for instance, if the school wants to improve the reputation of its music department), but will not assist others. As a result, some schools, depending on the resources available and their financial aid policies, may expect you to pay more than the EFC.

Let us look at an example: If your daughter's education costs total $15,000 per year, for example, and your EFC is $5,000 per year, then a four-year stay at the college should, in theory, cost you just $20,000 (4 × $5,000). What about the remaining $10,000 per year, though, that is not covered? That cost should be paid for, again, in theory, through financial aid such as student loans, scholarships, grants, and work-study programs. However, it may not be. (That is why I keep saying in theory.) The federal government's support for higher education has not matched the rising costs of education in recent years, so the financial aid system does not always work as it should. Even if your daughter qualifies for need-based financial aid, it is possible that the particular school that she wants to attend may not have enough funds to cover her need (or the school may simply not want to cover all of her need). Schools are under no obligation to meet 100 percent of your financial need.

Here is what could happen: Your daughter is offered a financial aid package consisting of loans and work-study, totaling $6,000. But that is not enough, you say? You now have an unmet need of $4,000 ($10,000 − $6,000). When this divide occurs in financial aid, you have what is known as a *financial aid gap*, explains Loewe. Your family then must come up with more money than your EFC to pay the college bill, he says. Some parents resolve the gap issue by taking out a federal PLUS loan, or, if possible, picking another college that has enough money to meet the family's full need.

In addition to federal and/or state aid, you may also qualify for need-based aid from the college itself. (In most cases, to be considered for this type of aid, you will need to fill out the Profile form in addition to the FAFSA.) Colleges offer the same types of aid that the government does: grants, loans, scholarships, and work-study. Some colleges will be able to offer you more than other colleges simply because they have larger endowments. How much you will actually get from a particular school will vary from one university to another. Some schools, for instance, have their own loan programs. Other schools offer work-study opportunities that, unlike the federal work-study options, are not based on need. Any student who wants to work, basically, can. However, because funds are limited; the amount awarded to you may fall short of the amount for which you are eligible.

In the end, even if you qualify for aid, you will have to compare schools dollar for dollar to see which institution offers the better deal. In some cases, you could pay less to attend an expensive college than to go to a cheaper state school. How is that? Let us look at that earlier example. You have an EFC of $5,000. Tuition at a state college costs $15,000 each year. You are eligible for $6,000 in federal financial aid, which leaves you with an unmet need of $4,000. One year at the state school, then, will cost you $9,000 (EFC of $5,000 + unmet need of $4,000), plus your federal loans. Suppose your child also wanted to attend a private college that costs twice the price, $30,000 per year. You still have the same EFC of $5,000, and you are still eligible for the same $6,000 in federal aid. The school really wants your kid, so it decides to meet all of your financial need. The final cost to you: just your EFC of $5,000 (plus the same amount in federal loans). When you compare the two schools, it is actually costing you $4,000 less!

This is just an example, of course. I do not mean to imply that more expensive, private schools will meet all of your financial need and less expensive, public schools will not. You have to do the math. When you compare aid packages, it may still cost less to attend a state school than a pricier private school. Or it may cost more (as in our example), or it may not cost that much more than you are paying for a state school to attend a private school.

Your EFC

At most public colleges, your EFC *is* determined by:

- Family income
- Accumulated savings
- Amount of taxes paid
- Family size
- The number of children attending college simultaneously
- The student's own savings

... but *is not* determined by:

- The parent's retirement assets such as a 401(k) or an IRA
- The family home

More Income Means Less Financial Aid

Do you qualify for aid? Consider these guidelines from the College Board:

If your income is	Financial Aid Options
Under $25,000	Eligible for need-based grants and other assistance
$25,000 to $75,000	Usually qualify for some need-based financial assistance (more loans than grants as income rises), but will also be expected to make a significant contribution
Over $75,000	Most likely will have to rely on personal loans and resources, including savings

Source: Copyright 2001 by College Entrance Examination Board and collegeboard.com. Reprinted with permission. All rights reserved.

Special Circumstances

Although the process of determining a student's eligibility for federal student aid is basically the same for all applicants, there is some flexibility. In some cases, your financial aid administrator may adjust your child's cost of attendance or the information used to calculate your EFC to take into account circumstances that might affect the amount you and your family are expected to contribute toward your child's education (see "Negotiating a Better Package"). These circumstances could include a family's unusual medical expenses. Also, an adjustment may be made if you or your spouse have been recently unemployed. Check with your school's financial aid administrator if you feel that you have such special circumstances. Keep in mind, however, that you will need adequate proof to support any adjustments.

If you want to get an early estimate of what the government thinks you can afford to pay for your education, try FinAid's Financial Aid Estimation Form (*www.finaid.org/calculators/finaidestimate.phtml*). It lets you play what-if games to give you an idea how changes in income and assets affect your EFC.

Understanding the Financial Aid Forms

To apply for federal and state student aid grants or loans, you must fill out the FAFSA. (A sample copy of this form is included at the end of this chapter.) You can fill out this form by hand and mail it in, or you can apply electronically from a PC (or a Mac that is equipped with a support browser) using *FAFSA on the web.* The web option gives you an automatic calculation of your EFC.

DOES YOUR FAMILY QUALIFY FOR FINANCIAL AID?

To get a better idea if you are likely to get aid and, if so, how much, consider the following factors, suggests the Department of Education:

Your child attends an expensive college. Generally, the more expensive the college, the more financial aid you can qualify for. In some cases, if your child decides to go to a more expensive college, you may actually end up paying less. This is because many expensive colleges have more funds to help students. Do not automatically assume that you cannot afford the more expensive college.

You have other children in college at the same time. If circumstances make it harder for your family to pay, financial aid often helps make up the difference. For most families, putting two children through college simultaneously without more financial aid would be much harder.

You have a large family. If you have several children who are still dependent upon you for support, the financial aid system will take that into account.

You pay above average state or local taxes. Some places have higher taxes than others do. This, too, is taken into account when awarding aid.

You have little accumulated wealth or savings. The financial aid system assumes that some of your savings ought to be used to pay for college. However, if you have not managed to save much money or accumulate other assets (such as stocks or bonds, for example), you may be more likely to qualify for aid or receive more aid.

You have unusual expenses such as medical bills. The financial aid system will take into account your increased need for aid if you have been faced with unusually large medical bills.

Your child does not work while attending college. Students often find that they can work part-time when attending college full-time. If your child does, she will be expected to contribute some of her earnings to pay for college.

You are willing to borrow. Loans are a big part of the financial aid package offered to many students. However, you do not have to accept loans; you can substitute your own money for the loan amount you may be offered.

If many of these factors apply to your family, then your chances of getting aid are higher than average for your income group. If few of these factors apply to your family, then the reverse is true; lower chances for aid and lower aid awards would be more typical.

Source: From *Managing the Price of College: A Handbook for Students and Families.*

As its name implies, this application is processed at no cost to you. Even if you think that you will not qualify for federal or state aid, you should still fill out a FAFSA. Why? Some colleges use the FAFSA to determine eligibility for their own institutional aid. At other colleges, you have to be rejected for federal aid before the school will consider giving you institutional aid. When private colleges dole out their institutional funds, though, they often want more information than is supplied on the FAFSA. As a result, many private schools will ask you to fill out an additional financial aid form. In most cases, that is the College Scholarship Service (CSS) Profile (CSS is the financial aid division of the College Board) or, in some cases, the school may have its own forms. When you are asked to fill out these other forms, you must do it *in addition to the FAFSA*. It is not one or the other.

What are the major differences between the FAFSA and the Profile? According to FinAid.org, they are:

- *Submission dates.* The CSS Profile can be submitted in the fall. FAFSA cannot be submitted before January 1.
- *Specific questions.* The CSS Profile contains questions specific to the school or program you are applying to. FAFSA contains the same questions for everyone.
- *Different methodology.* The CSS Profile determines your financial need differently than the FAFSA. The Profile considers equity in your home to be an asset (the FAFSA does not), taking into account such factors as whether your family owns a home. In general, the CSS Profile asks more detailed questions about your family's finances than the FAFSA does.
- *Minimum student contribution.* The CSS Profile requires this; the FAFSA does not.
- *Greater reliance on professional judgment.* The CSS Profile gives financial aid counselors greater freedom to grant aid based on a student's particular circumstances.
- *Cost.* The CSS Profile costs $5 ($6 if you register over the phone), plus $15 for each school or scholarship program selected. The FAFSA is free.

When Should You Apply?

As soon as possible. Many schools award financial aid to applicants in the order in which they receive the applications. So mail your applications early. For the FAFSA, you should apply as soon after January 1, of the year that your child

---

WHERE CAN I PICK UP FINANCIAL AID FORMS?

You can get a FAFSA from:

- Your high school guidance office
- A college financial aid office
- A local public library
- The Federal Student Aid Information Center: 800-433-3243
- Online at *www.fafsa.ed.gov* (step-by-step instructions are provided on this site.) If you have technical questions about using FAFSA on the web, call 1-800-801-0576.

You can get a Profile from:

- A college financial aid office
- Online at *www.collegeboard.org*
- Profile information line at 800-239-5888

---

expects to enter college, as possible. (For the school year 2003 to 2004, for example, you should apply soon after January 1, 2003.) You cannot apply *before* this date, however, so do not sign, date, or send your application before January 1. You must apply by July 1, and in some cases, even earlier than that. The federal government sets the July deadline, but schools and states may have their own, often earlier, deadlines for aid.

You need to apply for aid just once per school year, but you must reapply for federal aid every year. That means you must submit the FAFSA every year that you want aid. After you have applied for the first time, you might be able to apply more easily and quickly in subsequent years by simply completing a Renewal FAFSA. A Renewal FAFSA, fortunately, has fewer questions to answer. You have to fill out or update only the information that changed from the previous year. (There is also a renewal version of FAFSA on the web.) Federal aid does not necessarily follow you from one school to the next, though. Should you decide to switch schools midyear, make sure you find out (from your new school) how to continue receiving aid.

What Happens after You Apply?

Once your completed application is received by the processing system, the processor will produce a Student Aid Report (SAR). The SAR will report the information from your application, and if there are no questions or problems with the application, your SAR will report your EFC. Again, that is the number used in determining your eligibility for federal student aid. Your EFC will appear in the upper right-hand corner of your SAR. The results will be sent to you and to the schools that your child listed on his application:

- If you apply by mail, it will take about four weeks for your application to be processed and for you to receive a SAR in the mail.
- If you apply on the web, it will take about two weeks to receive a SAR.
- If the school submits your application electronically for you, it will take about one week to process your application.

If more than four weeks have passed since you submitted your FAFSA and you have not heard anything yet, you can check on your application through the FAFSA web site at *www.fafsa.ed.gov* (even if you did not apply electronically). You can also check by calling the Student Aid Information Center toll-free number (800-433-3243).

Once you receive your SAR, check it carefully for mistakes. You can fix any mistakes by putting the correct answer on the SAR, signing it, and mailing it back. Or, your school might be able to process corrections electronically for you. Make sure that you keep a photocopy of your SAR, should questions arise in the future.

You will get your financial aid news shortly after you get a letter of acceptance from the college. At this point, you will have to evaluate all of the offers received and decide what to do. It is easy to compare the schools financially: After aid and your EFC is considered, how much is each school costing you? Bear in mind, of course, that this is just the financial side of the college decision. Although money (or lack thereof) will certainly influence your choice of schools, it is not the only factor. You should also think about the academic record of the school and your child's needs, talents, and personality.

Improving Your Aid Eligibility

Improve your chances of getting aid. You can legitimately boost your chances of getting need-based financial aid simply by saving and spending your money smarter. Here are some of the most common financial planning strategies:

Make your debt work for you. As you have seen from the forms themselves, debt does not figure into the financial aid picture. No one cares if you have a car loan, credit card debt, or a mortgage. You will be expected to make the same contribution as those families who do not have this debt. Yet it is probably much tougher for you to come up with the required funds than the debt-free family because a portion of your income is needed to pay off your debts. No one said this financial aid formula was perfect! (At the many private schools that do consider home equity, however, this is *not* true. Having

THE TOP TEN TIPS FOR COMPLETING THE FAFSA

1. Have the following documents and information available when completing the FAFSA:

   - The most recent year's tax forms (or end-of-year pay stubs).
   - W-2 forms.
   - Records of the most recent year's untaxed income, such as child support and untaxed income from agencies such as Social Services, Social Security, and the Veterans Administration. (You do not need to send copies of these documents with your FAFSA, but you will need to refer to them when you file.)
   - The student's social security number (Be sure to copy the number correctly.).

2. Read instructions carefully, even if you have completed this form previously. The form itself may have been updated.

3. Do not leave blanks for any questions that require a numeric figure, such as a dollar amount or a test score. If your answer to a question is zero, be sure to write 0. If the question asks for your net worth, give the amount as of the day you complete the FAFSA form.

4. For dependent students, it is important that both the student and the parent(s) complete the FAFSA together. If the financial aid office has questions, they will contact the student first. It is imperative that both the student and parent(s) are aware of the information provided.

5. If you are completing the form for your child, be sure to complete a separate FAFSA application for each student. Check that the social security number reported is for the student filing the form. Incorrect social security numbers delay processing.

6. The asset questions pertaining to net value are for secondary and investment real estate only. Do not report the net value of your primary residence.

7. Check figures and calculations. Mistakes delay the processing of up to 40 percent of all forms processed.

8. Obtain the federal school code from the school or schools your child may be interested in attending.

9. Sign the FAFSA. Both the student and parent (if applicable) must sign and date this form.

10. File early, but do *not* sign, date, or mail the FAFSA before January 1. By filing early, you may receive favorable consideration for campus-based aid. You must file a FAFSA every year. Any changes in your family situation should be conveyed to your financial aid administrator. They might affect your eligibility.

Source: Scholarships.com. Reprinted with permission.

a mortgage in this situation is advantageous because it reduces the value of the asset.) To even the playing field, you could use your savings and investments (which do count in financial aid land) to pay down your car loan and other consumer debt. As a result, you might qualify for more aid because you have reduced your assets and (probably) your EFC.

Spend, spend, spend your cash. Liquid investments, like bank accounts and mutual funds (but not retirement funds), count as assets. The more assets your family has, the less need you have of financial assistance. You can lower your family's assets, then, by using some of your cash well before you fill out that financial aid application to buy big-ticket items like computers or cars. This strategy only makes sense, of course, if you were planning on buying these items anyway. Spending money unnecessarily is never a good strategy, and in this case, it will not save you that much money.

Spend, spend, spend your child's money. If possible, spend the assets in your child's name first. Why? Assets in a child's name are tapped more heavily than assets held in a parent's name. Kids are expected to kick in 35 percent of their own assets; for parents' funds, it is just 5.6 percent. (See Chapter 3 for a full explanation.) Unfortunately, you cannot simply drain your child's account. You must spend the money on legitimate expenses, such as summer camp or piano lessons, that will directly benefit the child. (A family car would not count, for instance, but you could buy a car for the child to drive himself.)

Save for retirement. Spend down your assets by contributing as much as you can to a 401(k) or other similar, tax-deferred account. Retirement funds are generally excluded from financial aid calculations.

Time your capital gains. Capital gains earned from the sale of stock or a home, for example, count as both income and assets. If you need to cash in such investments to help pay your college tab, try to sell those assets the year *before* your financial aid is calculated, or, if you can wait, in your child's senior year of college after aid has been figured for the year. (See the "Which Numbers Count" section.)

Which Numbers Count?

Financial aid is doled out on a yearly basis. That means you have to apply for aid every year, but which numbers count and for which year? The aid that you get in any given year is based on your income and assets of the previous tax year. Thus, if your child is going to college directly after high school, the amount of aid that you receive will depend on your financial situation the year before your child goes off to college. Her senior year of high school, then? Not exactly. When talking about finances and taxes, the year used is the *calendar* year, not the

Financial Aid from Your Home State

In the last few years, need-based student financial aid has been significantly increased in Georgia, Indiana, Missouri, Oklahoma, and, perhaps most dramatically, California. There, the Cal Grant program is expected to double in the next six years, from $530 million to $1.2 billion per year, explains William Trombley, senior editor at the National Center for Public Policy in Higher Education. In the past, many high school graduates who were eligible for Cal Grants did not receive them because the money ran out. In the 2000 to 2001 academic year, for example, 136,022 students were eligible, but only 57,254 received new awards.

The new law makes Cal Grants an entitlement program, like Medicare or Social Security. Every student who meets income criteria and who graduates with a 3.0 grade point average, says Trombley, is eligible for full tuition and fee payments at the state's public colleges and universities, and up to $9,708 to attend a private institution. The law requires the state to provide enough money for all eligible graduates.

The state higher education agency in your home state (listed in Chapter 6) can give you information about state aid, including aid from the Leveraging Educational Assistance Partnership (LEAP) Program, which is funded jointly by individual states and the U.S. Department of Education.

school year. (The calendar year runs from January to December, while the school year runs from September to June.) If little Johnny is starting college in September of 2004, then the year that will be used (for financial aid purposes) is 2003, which begins not in his senior year of high school, *but in his junior year*.

January to May, 2003 = Last half of junior year

September to December, 2003 = First half of senior year

So, if you are planning on boosting your chances of securing financial aid by using money in your child's account to get the money out of his name or selling off some stock that has risen in value (and taking some capital gains now), the time to make those maneuvers is before December 31 of your child's junior year of high school. Also, keep in mind that the amount you are awarded in aid that first year may not remain constant through your child's four years at school. You could wind up getting less in subsequent years because you or your spouse get a raise or promotion (which raises your income); you have substantial capital gains from an asset sold to help pay for college; one of your other children graduates from college, so you now only have one kid in school instead of two and other such factors.

HOW DOES YOUR STATE MEASURE UP?

Measuring Up 2002, the first report card that grades the states on their performance in higher education, was recently published by the independent, nonpartisan National Center for Public Policy and Higher Education in San Jose, California. Although the report card was developed primarily to give legislators objective information to assess and improve higher education, there is one measure of performance that should be of interest to parents: affordability. That is, how affordable is higher education in each state?

According to the findings of this report, people in some states have to pay a much higher share of their income to attend college. In New York, for instance, tuition, room, and board (less financial aid) at public four-year colleges and universities require about 30 percent of family income. In Wisconsin, it accounts for about 18 percent of family income. Affordability, in this analysis, depends primarily on tuition levels and room and board at the various kinds of schools in the state and on the level of financial aid provided to students and their families.

Each state is evaluated, using A through F grades in five key areas. The following describes the excerpted grade and analysis of the affordability measure. For more information about Measuring Up 2002, visit *www.highereducation.org*.

	PERCENT OF INCOME NEEDED TO PAY FOR COLLEGE EXPENSES MINUS FINANCIAL AID:		
STATE	AT COMMUNITY COLLEGES	AT PUBLIC 4-YEAR COLLEGES	AT PRIVATE 4-YEAR COLLEGES
Alabama	21%	23%	44%
Alaska	20%	21%	32%
Arizona	24%	25%	54%
Arkansas	17%	20%	39%

Source: National Center for Public Policy and Higher Education. Reprinted with permission.

How Does Financial Aid Work in Cases of Divorce?

The financial aid application should be completed by the custodial parent. Public institutions will look at just the custodial parent's finances when calculating how much aid they will give. However, if the parent you receive financial support from has remarried, your stepparent's financial information is required on the FAFSA. This does not mean that your stepparent is obligated to give financial assistance to you, but his or her income and assets represent significant information about the family's resources. The government wants to know that when making financial aid decisions. Private schools are not bound by federal financial regulations. They may ask for information about the noncustodial parent, too. They may factor in both parents' incomes, even if there is little chance that the noncustodial parent will chip in. In addition, if one or both parents has remarried, some private colleges will take the stepparents' finances into account, too. All of this probably means that getting financial aid is just that much more difficult if you and your spouse split up.

Ask the Financial Aid Officer

Check out the dorms, the dining hall, and the library. Are the professors highly regarded? Is the curriculum inspired? Is campus life lively? Too lively to get any studying done? When picking a college for your child, you must, naturally, check out all of these elements. However, when you are taking the campus tour, do not forget to swing by the financial aid office. Financial aid packages vary from one college to another and from one year to the next at the *same* college, depending on the number of students applying, the financial needs of those applicants, and the resources of the college itself. What should you hope to learn exactly from this visit? You want to find out how much the total cost of attendance is (including room and board) as well as the school's policies and procedures regarding financial aid. The school may have some literature to offer on the subject, which may answer many of your questions. If not, ask someone in the financial aid office itself. Some questions that you might want to ask include:

- What financial aid programs are available at your school? Is it need-based aid, merit-based aid, and/or scholarships?
- Is this aid just for freshmen? How does aid differ for sophomores and upperclassmen? (Some schools offer more scholarship money to freshmen, for example. By junior and senior years, that scholarship money might become loans or a work-study arrangement.)
- How do you determine if a family qualifies for aid? What are the requirements?
- What financial aid forms must I fill out? The FAFSA and the Profile?
- Will my need affect my child's chances of getting accepted at the school? (This question requires clarification so please see the "Is the College Need Blind?" section.)
- Will the school meet 100 percent of our family's financial need?
- What happens if my child is eligible for aid and then receives a scholarship from a source other than the college? Will the college simply replace a loan or grant that my child would have received from the school?
- When will we be notified about our eligibility for financial aid?

Is the School Need Blind?

In the past, schools were *need blind*. That is, the decision to admit a student (or not) to the college was made without regard to the student's ability to pay. A student's need for financial aid simply was not a factor in the admissions process. (That was the ideal, anyway.) Unfortunately, that practice is becoming less prevalent, especially at the most expensive private schools.

"Admissions and financial aid are no longer separate functions, but one combined function called enrollment management," says Philip C. Johnson, a financial planner in Clifton, New York, who specializes in college planning. "Your financial need can influence your ability to be admitted to a college." Outstanding candidates, of course, will be admitted no matter what, but the more average Joes? A student may or may not be admitted, depending on how much Mommy and Daddy can afford to pay, says Johnson. The result? Your child might be put on a waiting list—or worse, rejected—because he or she is going to cost the school too much money.

Wait a minute. Let us assume that a college is considering two equally qualified applicants. Does this mean that the school may accept the student who is *not* requesting financial aid over the student who does? Yes. Does that further mean that you should not apply for financial aid in the hopes that you will beat out some other kid who does request aid? Nope. Unless you are expecting a windfall from the grandparents (or the latest hot stock tip), you still have to come up with the cash to pay that college tab. (Yes, you can borrow an enormous amount of money for college, but remember: You have to pay all of that money back, with interest.) It seems pointless, then, to forgo possible aid just to get your son accepted into Harvard if, ultimately, you have to turn down the offer because you cannot afford to send him there. A better strategy: Apply for financial aid, and apply to a range of schools. Who knows? One of the Ivy League schools may come through for you. Or a less prestigious school (but one with a good reputation) may offer you a very affordable deal that will not break your budget for years to come.

Negotiating a Better Package

You have just received your financial aid award letter in the mail, but your elation soon cools after you read that the amount offered is $5,000 less than the amount you need. If you are unhappy with the financial aid package you have received, you can try to negotiate the offer, but you must do it *nicely*. (Threatening to send your child to another school unless the college ups its offer does not work. In fact, it may cause the financial aid officer *not* to help you find more aid dollars.) Also, you must be prepared for the school to say no. Some schools will not negotiate.

Once you get the award letter (and see that the school has not met your need), call the school's financial aid officer and make an appointment to see him. If possible, you really should try to do this in person rather than on the telephone because it is easier to negotiate face to face, he says, and harder for the other person to say no. When you make that initial call, do not say that you are unhappy with the package or even that you want to *negotiate*. Instead, say that you want to *review* your package.

Now, what do you say at this meeting? You do not want to appear too aggressive. You are not a huckster, trying to cut a deal. Rather, your family has a need, and it is not being met. Explain that the financial aid forms simply do not ask questions about everything, and you have some issues that make your family's financial situation a bit different. You will want to bring proof of as much of this untapped ammunition as possible. Some legitimate situations include:

- *You or your spouse recently lost a job*. If either partner was recently downsized, fired, or forced to take early retirement and is now unemployed, you probably have a perfectly valid reason to appeal an aid package.

- *You have unusually high medical bills*. Perhaps you are caring for a frail parent who requires in-home or even nursing care that is not covered by insurance.

- *You have other education bills to pay*. Private school tuition for younger siblings and graduate school tuition for older siblings are not included on the financial aid forms, yet this can substantially cut into the income available to pay for college.

- *Your annual income is typically lower*. Perhaps you or your spouse's bonus was bigger than normal last year. (You will need tax returns from previous years to prove this.) Your income affects your EFC, and most schools cannot change that figure, but they may be able to meet all of your needs and not leave a gap. (You will still have to pay the higher EFC, of course, at least until next year, when your income is back to a more typical level.)

- *You have a lot of debt*. No financial aid officer will consider your mortgage, of course, to be a plausible reason to beef up your aid package. However, if you have racked up a lot of credit card debt or even a second mortgage or home equity line of credit to pay medical or other legitimate bills (vacations or a new car, for instance, will not win you any sympathy), you might have a chance. Again, you will need proof to back up such claims.

Finally, you should probably bring up a better offer that your child received from another school. (We say probably because it depends on the situation.) Obviously, you will want to do this tactfully. Do not try to play Can You Top This? Some schools may match the better offer (but not beat it). Some schools, though, will not even talk to you about an offer from another school because they feel it is like comparing apples and oranges. This method works best, of course, if you are talking about two comparable schools and if your child has not already been accepted. If the school knows that your child plans on attending no matter how much they award in financial aid, are they really going to work hard to cut you a better deal? Your chances of getting more aid are better if you say that the decision of your child's admission may rest on the aid received. Ultimately, the ability to negotiate your financial aid package may rest on how much the school wants your child. "If a student is attractive to a college," Raymond Loewe, "that college will not want to lose the student due to lack of money."

CHAPTER 8

The Search for Scholarship Money

Mention the word scholarship to the parents of college-age kids and you will likely hear a mouthful. These parents will either cite statistics about the country's huge scholarship pool, a large chunk of which goes unclaimed simply because students, parents, and counselors are unaware that such funds even exist. (These are generally the parents of kids who get scholarships.) Or, they will pooh-pooh the whole idea, claiming that if your kid is not an Einstein or the next Wynton Marsalis, your child will be lucky to win enough to cover books, never mind tuition. (These are the parents whose children did not get scholarships.)

The truth, of course, lies somewhere in the middle. Some kids do win scholarships—from either the college itself or a private organization—that help cover the costs of tuition and room and board. And others? Well, they win a whopping $150. No matter how much money is received, a scholarship *is* money that you do not have to repay. This money is awarded to students based on merit and/or financial need. That is, merit scholarships are awarded because the student, for example, is an outstanding math student. The award has nothing to do with a family's financial need. Other scholarships, however, are awarded because the student, again, is a gifted mathematician, but his family also meets certain need criteria.

Still, you do not exactly get this money for nothing. In most cases, finding the particular scholarship(s) that you might qualify for—and then writing an essay and filling out the forms needed to apply for the award—takes time and energy (which, unless you have nothing else to do, costs money). So, yes, your child may get a free ride with a scholarship, but do not put all of your eggs into that basket because:

- *You have to fit the required profile—exactly.* Only green-eyed students who live in Oshkosh, Wisconsin and plan to study molecular biology need apply? That is a bit far-fetched, of course, but most kids simply do not meet the requirements needed for many private scholarships. To receive the Gloria Fecht Memorial Scholarship money, for example, an applicant must be a girl, live in Southern California, prove financial need, have a minimum 3.0 GPA, and be interested in golf! To qualify for the Beckley Scholarship at Juniata College in Huntingdon, PA, students must be left-handed. To receive a scholarship from the Welsh Guild, students must be of Welsh decent and live within 150 miles of Philadelphia (or plan to enroll in a college within that radius).

- *The money awarded, in many cases, is based on need and merit.* Do not assume that your child will get a scholarship just because she is gifted, talented, and scores high on the SAT. A majority of that scholarship money is *need-based,* says Linda Paras, president and CEO of the National Alliance for Excellence, an educational foundation that does offer scholarships to gifted and talented students irregardless of need. The scholarship may say it is for the best poet, says Paras, but often it is really for the *best poet with need.*

- *The money received in many cases is not all that much.* Many people will argue that money *is* money, especially when it is a free gift, and there is a certain prestige attached to winning a scholarship (no matter how small an amount the scholarship actually is). Still, it seems like it might be easier and more fun for your child to earn that same $750 with a part-time job than winning it through a scholarship.

- *The award may be even less than you think.* Before your child accepts any award, check to see if the scholarship is renewable. Some scholarship funds offer students a generous award for the first year, but reduce it for the subsequent years. In other cases, the same dollar amount is granted each year, but the award is granted one year at a time. That means, a student must reapply for the scholarship *every* year. In the case of an athletic scholarship, your son could lose his chance of renewing an award, for example, if he has a disagreement with his coach or he simply does not perform well on the playing field that year.

- *A scholarship may not actually save you any money.* That is right: *not save you any money.* How can that be? Some schools reduce any need-based grants or scholarships that they had planned on giving a student by the amount of private scholarship money (that is scholarship money received by any source outside the school itself) the student receives. In the end, you wind up paying the same amount, with or without the scholarship. Some schools, however, will let you use the scholarship money to reduce your Expected Family Contribution (EFC) or to replace loans. Brown University in Providence, Rhode Island, for example, lets you deduct an outside scholarship award from the student's loans. A growing number of schools will let you use scholarship money to fill in the gaps. (Despite the financial aid package it offers you, schools do not always fill 100 percent of your family's need. The amount that is unmet is known as the *financial aid gap*.) Obviously, these latter situations are ideally how you want the scholarship money to be used.

The Search Begins

It is sort of like finding a needle in a haystack, but a lot more exciting because that needle could be worth $50,000 or more. Here is how to get a successful scholarship search underway:

- *Do an online search.* Search engines, such as the ones listed in the following, can help you find what is out there fast.
  - *www.collegeboard.org*   The College Board has a scholarship search called *Fund Finder*, a database of private and public scholarships and grants. Many libraries and school guidance offices offer this service. (It is always free of charge because students *cannot* be charged for using Fund Finder.)
  - *www.scholarships.com*   This free college scholarship search service will compare your child's profile to a database of approximately 600,000 college scholarships worth more than $1.4 billion from over 8,000 sources. The scholarship awards that match your child's profile will be available to you online immediately.
  - *www.fastweb.com*   Another free scholarship search service that is linked to more than 600,000 scholarships worth over $1 billion.
  - *www.collegenet.com/mach25*   This web site, which was launched in 1995, offers the Mach25, which it claims is the fastest free scholarship search on the web, searching a database of over 600,000 scholarships totaling over $1.6 billion. In addition, the site lets you complete, file, and pay for your college admissions application entirely through the Internet. The search engine lets you pick a college, or at least narrow down your choices, by region, college sports, major, tuition, and other criteria. You can then review, compare, and sort schools.
  - *www.srnexpress.com*   The Scholarship Resource Network Express is a database of over 8,000 programs with a distribution level of over

150,000 awards for undergraduate and post-graduate students worth more than $35 million.

- *Go to the library*. Why waste your time with this sluggish old dinosaur when you have got access to the fleet-footed web? You will find a host of good, useful scholarship guides available, just brimming with information about every type of scholarship, ranging from the big-name, big-dollar awards (listed at the end of this chapter) to the smaller, more obscure awards. Before you start to page through these tomes, though, be sure that you have the latest edition (if you are using a book like Peterson's *Scholarships, Grants and Prizes*, for instance, which is revised every year) because this type of information changes constantly. Do not waste your time reading last year's book that probably includes some outdated (and thus, possibly misleading) information. Some suggested reading:

  - *The Scholarship Book 2002: The Complete Guide to Private-Sector Scholarships, Fellowships, Grants, and Loans for the Undergraduate* by National Scholarship Research Service (Prentice Hall Press).
  - *How to Go to College Almost for Free* by Benjamin R. Kaplan (Waggle Dancer Books). This is a first-person account of how this student won $90,000 worth of merit-based scholarships.
  - *Winning Scholarships for College: An Insider's Guide* by Marianne Ragins (Owl Books).
  - *Peterson's Scholarships, Grants and Prizes 2003* (Peterson's Guides).
  - *The Complete Scholarship Book: The Biggest, Easiest Guide for Getting the Most Money for College* by Fastweb.com (Sourcebooks Trade).
  - There are a handful of other books that focus on certain fields of study such as *Peterson's Professional Degree Programs in the Visual Performing Arts* (Peterson's Guides) and *Scholarships and Loans for Nursing Education* by Regina Fawcett (National League for Nursing).
  - *Kaplan Scholarships 2003* by David Weber (Kaplan).

- *Get information from school*. When it comes to scholarships (and most college preparation, for that matter), high school guidance counselors can be a help or a hindrance. It really depends. Some guidance counselors are so knowledgeable and so helpful that you just want to clone them and send them out to every school across America, says Brian E. Glickman, a certified public accountant who runs Tuition Solutions, a college planning firm, in Smithtown, New York. "Others?" he says. "Let's just say they're not quite as helpful." In most high schools, though, you can expect the *guidance office* to at least have a list of scholarships, both local and national. The guidance counselor may even have some of the applications. If not, you will have to write or call the organization offering the scholarship and have the application and other relevant material mailed to you.

The financial aid office at the college itself may be able to help you, too. Ask if the school offers any scholarships, and, if so, what the requirements are. Find out if you need to apply separately for these scholarships or if the school simply doles them out based on the student's college admissions application. Finally, ask the financial aid officer how the school treats outside scholarships. (Some schools actually give this information on their web site, but most do not.) If the school reduces its own grant money by the amount of the scholarship, you could try to cut a better deal. To improve your chances of success, get the scholarship provider involved, if you can. Obviously, these providers carry more clout than one parent pleading his child's case.

- Use a computerized service—*not*. Why pay someone to do this for you when you can do it yourself? These services, which are advertised online and in campus newspapers, are not cheap (fees run about $200, but can exceed $1,000), and you may end up with a list of awards that your child has no chance of winning (see the following Scholarship Scams section). You probably will not glean any information from these services that you will not learn on your own through a web search, a visit to the library, or a conversation with your child's guidance counselor.

Show Me the Money

Maybe your child is a scholar, the next Michael Jordan, a talented sculptor, a virtuoso musician, or none of these. There is scholarship money out there, but you have to know where to look. Private scholarships are offered by almost every organization under the sun, including for-profit companies, professional groups, unions, community organizations, and religious groups. The following are some possibilities.

Your Employer

Many corporations, as well as labor unions, offer scholarships and other programs to help pay the cost of college for employees' or members' children. The Kohler Company, for instance, hands out 15 $1,500 awards per year, based on a student's academic performance. (These awards are renewable for up to three additional years.) Similarly, the Gerber Products Company (yes, the baby food people) award college-bound kids of employees $1,500 per year, if the students have a strong academic record and demonstrate leadership skills. (The amount is renewable for up to three additional years.) The International Brotherhood of Teamsters awards 75 scholarships per year, 25 of which are worth $25,000, to dependent children of Teamster members. Many, many, many companies and unions offer similar deals. Although these programs are heavily promoted by the company or union, check with your human resources department or your local union representative to find out what your job offers (if you have not heard of such deals) and to get the details. Application deadlines vary from one company's program to the next, as do academic requirements. At Gerber, for instance, students must maintain a C average once they get to college if they hope to renew their scholarship.

Professional Organizations

If your child is one of those students who already knows that he would like to study physics, engineering, or accounting in college, you may be able to get some scholarship money from an organization connected with your child's field of interest. The American Physical Society, for example, which is a professional society for physicists, offers scholarships to minority undergraduate students who plan to major in physics. The New Jersey Society of Certified Public Accountants Scholarship Fund offers awards, ranging from $500 to $1,500 per year, to students enrolling in college as accounting majors. To find professional groups affiliated with your child's desired profession, check out the Encyclopedia of Associations, a reference book that you will find in most libraries that lists the addresses and phone numbers of various associations across the country, or go online to the American Society of Association Executives (*www.asae.net.org*).

Your Home State

Some states offer scholarships and grants to residents who attend in-state schools. Georgia, for example, offers HOPE scholarships. (That stands for Helping Outstanding Pupils Educationally. Do not confuse this, however, with the Hope Scholarship tax credit discussed in Chapter 6.) These scholarships provide full tuition and fees at public campuses and $3,000 toward tuition and fees at private institutions. Who are the recipients? Georgia students who graduate from high school with at least a B average. More than 650,000 students in Georgia have been awarded these scholarships since they were introduced in 1993. What is more, the law was changed last year to enable HOPE scholarship winners to apply for federal Pell grants as well. In Maryland, residents who graduate in the top 1 percent of their class may win $1,500 per year, for up to four years. To learn about programs available in your state, contact your state agency (listed in Chapter 6).

Other Groups

The list here is almost endless. Your child may qualify for a scholarship, even if he is just an average student with no particular talents, simply because he (or you) can check yes next to one or more of the following groups:

- Religious affiliation
- Hobbies and special interests
- Extracurricular activities

- Local community and civic organizations
- Ethnic/racial background
- Women
- Minority
- Disabled

Here is a sampling of what is available: Community organizations and civic groups, such as the Elks, Kiwanis, Jaycees, American Legion, and Rotary International, offer thousands of dollars to promising students. The Elks National Foundation (773-755-4872, *www.elks.org*), for example, offers more than $3.3 million in college scholarships each year to graduating high school seniors. Not all recipients need to be children or grandchildren of Elks members. If your son or daughter is of Italian descent, try the Order Sons of Italy in America (202-547-5106, *www.osia.org*) that offers 10 to 14 scholarships of $4,000 to $25 annually. Native Americans who are members of the Cherokee Nation may qualify for one of the Nation's 900 scholarships awarded each semester. For hearing-impaired students, the EAR Foundation offers its Minnie Pearl Scholarship (800-545-HEAR, *www.earfoundation.org*), and the Pfizer Epilepsy Scholarship Award (800-292-7373, *www.epilepsy-scholarship.com*) is given to 16 to students who suffer from epilepsy. For the 2002–2003 academic year the Knights of Columbus (203-772-2130 *www.kofc.org*) awarded 128 scholarships, including 55 new $1,500 renewable scholarships, to children (of members) who are enrolling in Catholic colleges. The Executive Women International Scholarship Program (801-355-2800, *www.executivewomen.org*) awards up to $10,000 to 130 high school juniors, boys and girls, each year. Finally, students who can trace their John Hancock back to the original signers of the Declaration of Independence can compete for six to eight annual award of $1,200 to $1,500. (With all of these groups, some restrictions may apply. You must check with each organization for complete details about awards and eligibility requirements.)

When Your Child Is an Athlete

Full and partial scholarships are awarded to students based on their athletic ability. That is nothing new, but your kid does not necessarily have to be a football star to qualify. Schools do offer athletic scholarships for less high-profile sports like swimming, volleyball, lacrosse, even bowling and golf.

For some kids, though, winning an athletic scholarship is more than a means to pay for college. It is a means in itself. Athletic scholarships are often status symbols. There is something quasi-professional, after all, about being *recruited* by a college to play basketball on their team.

Just who gets these awards and how? Schools with top-level teams offer scholarships to the best high school and junior college athletes. (Again, no surprise there.) If your child is really a star—most likely in a sport like football or basketball that gets a lot of local newspaper coverage—you do not have to go looking for an athletic scholarship. The school will come to *you*, as schools regularly track the performance records of potential prospects. However, if your daughter is not exactly star material or if she plays a less popular sport, she will have to hunt down an athletic scholarship just as she would any other scholarship.

To do so, she needs to contact the coach of the sport that she plays *in writing*. (This way, your child's letter will be on record for future reference.) She should ask her present coach to write a letter of recommendation and include it with her letter. If the college coach is interested, he or she will probably want your daughter to visit the school in person. It is unusual for a coach to recommend a student for a scholarship if he or she has not seen the student athlete perform. Even if your daughter does not win a scholarship through such efforts, she may still walk away with a more attractive financial aid package. Why? Coaches often work closely with the school's financial aid officers to strike a juicier deal for athletes they want.

Athletic scholarships are generally given on a one-year, renewable basis. The National Collegiate Athletic Association (NCAA) establishes rules and regulations for the various colleges and universities. These rules stipulate how many athletic awards a school can give out and in which sports. Schools are grouped into different divisions, and the rules vary, again, depending on the division the school is in. Nearly all of the Division I and I-AA (but not the Ivy League schools), for example, can and do offer full athletic scholarships. Division II schools tend to offer partial scholarships. Division III schools do not give any money at all, but they do recruit high school athletes to play on their teams.

Most sports in the NCAA use the equivalency method to hand out scholarships. Here is how it works: Each Division I school can award 18 full ice hockey scholarships, for example, per year. One of these schools could give 18 hockey players each a full scholarship, or, it could award 36 partial scholarships to 36 students, or it could grant any combination thereof, as long the amount of money given out totaled 18 full scholarships.

Sports that are classified as head count sports, though, do not adhere to equivalency rules. If the NCAA limit on a head count sport is the same 18 scholarships, let us say, then only 18 students will receive awards. It does not matter if the students receive partial or full scholarships: Only 18 students in a given year may receive scholarship money.

For more details on getting an athletic scholarship, you will want to check out these books:

- *Athletic Scholarships 4th Edition: Thousands of Grants and over $400 million for College-Bound Athletes* by Andy Clark and Amy Clark (Checkmark Books) is a state-by-state listing of four-year and two-year colleges and universities that offer athletic incentives to both male and female students.

- *Peterson's Sports Scholarships and College Athletic Programs* (Peterson's Guides).
- *The Athletic Recruiting and Scholarship Guide* by Wayne Mizzon (Mass Merkes Paperback).

SCHOLARSHIP SCAMS

Millions in unclaimed scholarship money! Guaranteed, or your money back! Advertisements that promise to help you find such funds for college are everywhere: the Internet, the newspaper, a brochure mailed to your home, or perhaps a flyer posted on your child's school bulletin board. Students are asked to fill out a questionnaire, and in return for a relatively small fee, the company will help you find a scholarship. Yeah, right.

Unfortunately, many of these scholarship companies are frauds, using official-looking logos and official-sounding names that include the words national or federal. In return for those fees of $200 or so (up to $1,500, in some cases), students do not get information on scholarships that match their skills and academic records, as promised. Instead, they get a one-size-fits-all list of college scholarships that the student could easily have attained himself from the Internet or the school guidance office and which he has little or no chance of getting. What about those guarantees? To get your money back, you actually have to apply for every scholarship on the list that the company's given you (or some other such condition buried in the fine print), making it nearly impossible to ever collect a refund.

The scams have become so pervasive in recent years, that the Federal Trade Commission (FTC) has begun cracking down on companies that promise scholarships in exchange for advance fees. (In several cases, the FTC has put the companies out of business.) Legitimate companies, says the FTC, do not promise scholarships. Some come-ons to steer clear of include:

- "The scholarship is guaranteed or your money back."
- "You cannot get this information anywhere else."
- "I just need your credit card or bank account number to hold this scholarship."
- "We will do all the work."
- "The scholarship will cost some money."
- "You are a finalist" in a scholarship competition you never entered.

To learn more about scholarship scams and how to avoid them, visit the following sites:

- Federal Trade Commission: *www.ftc.gov*, 202-FTC-HELP
- Better Business Bureau: *www.bbb.org*, 703-276-0100
- National Fraud Information Center: *www.fraud.org*, 800-876-7060

How To Apply for a Scholarship

No matter how gifted or talented your child is, most scholarships will not just arrive on your doorstep. You have to go after this money. As mentioned before: It takes a lot of time and effort, but if you do it right, the payoff can be quite large.

Start Early

It is never too early to start researching the kinds of scholarships that are available and for which you qualify. By junior year, in fact, your child should draw up a list various scholarships (that he feels he could possibly win) and contact those foundations for applications. Why so early? He needs time to fill out the application.

Read the Fine Print

What is the criteria for this scholarship? Does your child meet the requirements? Do not waste your time applying for a scholarship that your child does not qualify for. (It is hard enough to win a scholarship that she does qualify for.) In addition, find out how financial need figures into the equation. Although true scholarships are based purely on merit (and aid is meant for students with financial need), the lines are not that neatly drawn. The deciding factor when awarding a scholarship is often need, not merit.

Consider a Less-Prestigious School

If your child is setting his sights on an institutional merit scholarship (that is, a scholarship from the school itself based on the child's academic record or an outstanding talent), forget about the big-name schools. The more extraordinary the school, says Paras, the less likely it is that your child will get a merit scholarship. Instead, apply to schools that want what your child has. If a college is trying to build up the reputation of its music department, it will pay (in the form of scholarships) to get students who are outstanding musicians to attend.

Fill Out the Application Neatly and On Time

There are relatively few private scholarships based on pure merit (compared to those that are need-based), so the competition for these awards is keen. To insure that your application is reviewed, cross every T and dot every I. In many cases, the foundations will simply toss out an application that includes spelling errors or is not typed neatly. Ditto if your application is handed in after the deadline.

Take the Time Needed To Write a Strong Essay

Most scholarship programs ask you to write an essay about your goals or intended field of study. Because the essay is often a key component (and it takes some effort to write a really good essay), there is nothing wrong with using the same essay for different scholarships, if it is applicable. Include all aspects of your life, such as school, work, community service, sports, clubs, and so on that fit. Include anything that may be exceptional about you and your accomplishments.

Be Sure To Answer All of the Questions Asked

Leave something out and the scholarship people reading your application are not going to call you back to tell you, for example, that you only included two personal recommendations instead of the required three. They are busy people, wading through hundreds of applications like yours. What are they going to do with an incomplete application? Toss it out.

Follow up

Once you have mailed your application, follow up with a phone call to make sure that your application arrived and that you included all of the necessary information. Get the name and the title of the person that you speak to in case you need to prove later on that your application arrived on time or if there is a question about some aspect of your application.

Express Your Thanks

By now, you may have given up asking your kids to write thank-you notes for gifts received from far-flung relatives. If your child is lucky enough to win a scholarship, though, it is time to crack that letter-writing whip again. No matter how

---

TOP TEN REASONS AN APPLICATION WILL *NOT* WIN A SCHOLARSHIP

1. Mail the envelope without the application enclosed.
2. Submit an incomplete application.
3. Forget to include your name or address.
4. Submit an illegible or unintelligible application.
5. Send the appliction "postage due."
6. Submit irrelevant or inappropriate supporting documentation.
7. Submit a dirty or stained application.
8. Apply for an award when you clearly don't meet even the minimum requirements.
9. Make spelling errors.
10. Be rude or abusive to the judges.

Source: Scholarships.com. Reprinted with permission.

small the scholarship amount received, students should always write a thank-you note to the foundation or organization offering the award. (Seriously, folks, it is really bad form not to do so.) Of course, the note should be neat and free of typos and other errors.

A Scholarship Sampling

To give you an idea of what is available, some of the top scholarships and their requirements are listed in the following. To receive an application, please send an SASE to the following addresses or download an application from the web site listed:

Horace Mann Scholarships
One Horace Mann Plaza
Springfield, IL 62715
www.horacemann.com

One $10,000 scholarship, five $4,000 scholarships, and 20 $1,000 scholarships are awarded to high school students who are dependents of public school employees. Students must have at least a B average and score at least 23 on ACT or 1100 on SAT.

Deadline: February 28

National Alliance for Excellence
1070-H Highway 34, Suite 205
Matawar, NJ 07747
732-765-1730
www.excellence.org

About 100 scholarships, ranging from $1,000 to $5,000, are awarded to students for *superior* performance in the following areas, regardless of need: academic achievement, visual and/or performing arts, technological innovation. Winners are also given mentorship and internship opportunities with leading figures and companies throughout the country. Very, very competitive.

Deadline: None. You can apply at any time during the year

Intel Science Talent Search
Contact: Science Service
1719 N Street, NW
Washington, DC 20036-2888
202-785-2255
www.sciserv.org

Formerly sponsored by the Westinghouse Foundation, this highly regarded science contest for high school seniors has been sponsored by the Intel Corporation since 1998. One $100,000 scholarship, one $75,000, one $50,000, three $25,000, four $20,000, and 30 $5,000 scholarships are given to students who complete an original research project in physics, chemistry, engineering, or any other mathematics or science category. All finalists have the opportunity to meet more than 1,200 distinguished scientists, physicians, engineers, and mathematicians. About 2,000 high school students compete for these awards each year.

Deadline: Last week of November generally

Distributive Education Clubs of America (DECA)
1908 Association Drive
Reston, VA 20191-1594
703-860-5000
www.DECA.org

More than 30 awards of $1,000 are given to students who plan to study, marketing, merchandising, management, or marketing education. (The number of awards varies from one year to the next.) Some of these scholarships are tied to work experience. To qualify, students must be both active DECA members and employees of the sponsoring company such as Best Buy, Sears, and Winn-Dixie. The Food Marketing Institute offers scholarships to DECA members who are employed in the supermarket industry. Other scholarships, such as the ones offered by Otis Spunkmeyer and Harry A. Applegate, are based on scholastic record, DECA activity, community involvement, and leadership ability.

Deadline: Mid-February

William Randolph Hearst Foundation
United States Senate Youth Program
90 New Montgomery Street
Suite 1212
San Francisco, CA 94105-4504
800-841-7048
www.ussenateyouth.org

One hundred and four $5,000 scholarships are awarded to high school seniors and juniors who hold an elected office in their school's student government. (These scholarships are given to two students in each state plus the District of Columbia and the Department of Defense Education Activity. Although the Hearst Foundation funds this program, selection of scholarship winners is made by the head of the Department of Education in each state.) An added perk: Winners attend the U.S. Senate Youth Program's Washington Week, in which they get to see the national government in action. (All expenses, including air fare and hotel accommodations, are paid for by the Hearst Foundation.)

Deadline: Early fall, generally; varies by state

Western Golf Association
Evans Scholars Foundation
1 Briar Road
Golf, IL 60029
847-724-4600
www.westerngolfassociation.com

According to the foundation's literature, this is the largest privately funded college scholarship program in the nation. About 200 full tuition and housing awards called the Chick Evans Caddie Scholarships are given each year. To qualify, students must have caddied for two years or more, rank among the top 25 percent of their high school class, be of outstanding personal character, and show financial need. Almost all Evans Scholars attend one of the 14 universities where the foundation maintains a chapter house.

Deadline: September 30 of senior year

National Foundation for Advancement in the Arts
Arts Recognition and Talent Search (ARTS)
800 Brickell Avenue, Suite 500
Miami, FL 33131
www.ARTSawards.org

Each year, thousands of kids apply to ARTS, a national program that is widely acknowledged as the most prestigious award program for the arts and creative writing in the country. ARTS does not offer scholarships per se, but cash awards, ranging from $100 to $3,000, which the foundation hopes students will use for college. High school seniors (and other 17- and 18-year-old artists) compete in the performing, visual, and literary arts. Three $25,000 awards are then given to kids who won at the $3,000 level. (Students can win more than one award.) Twenty finalists from the ARTs program are designated Presidential Scholars in the Arts and although there is no cash award for this honor, this designation often leads to scholarship offers from colleges themselves. "It's the kiss of success," says Beth Czeskleba, the foundation's director of communications. Winners attend the all-expense-paid Presidential Scholars National Recognition Week in Washington, D.C., where they meet with elected representatives, authors, musicians, and other accomplished people.

Deadline: October 1 for the application, November 1 for audition materials

National Merit Scholarship Corporation
1560 Sherman Avenue
Suite 200
Evanston, IL 60201
www.nationalmerit.org

This independent, not-for-profit organization offers college scholarships through its two programs: the National Merit Scholarship Program (open to all students) and the National Achievement Scholarship Program (awarded to outstanding Black American students). Winners receive $2,500. Additional scholarships are sponsored by various colleges and corporations.

Deadline: High school students enter this competition by taking the Preliminary SAT/National Merit Scholarship Qualifying Test (PSAT/NMSQT), usually when they are juniors

United Negro College Fund (UNCF)
8260 Willow Oak Corporate Drive
Fairfax, VA 22031
www.uncf.org

The United Negro College Fund awards scholarships to undergraduate and graduate students attending a UNCF member college as well as to those students attending other historically black colleges. Once a student receives a UNCF scholarship, it may be renewed in subsequent years if the student continues to meet eligibility requirements such as a minimum grade point average of 2.5 and unmet financial need. One example of these awards: The Merck/UNCF Science Initiative, which will offer 37 fellowships per year (for the next 10 years), is awarded to African American students pursuing careers in scientific research.

Deadline: Varies, depending on the particular scholarship

National Honor Society Scholarships
Contact: Your school's National Honor Society chapter or *www.nassp.org*

Each National Honor Society chapter may nominate two senior chapter members for this national scholarship. 200 scholarships of $1,000 each are awarded. To qualify, students must be high school seniors and a member of the National Honor Society.

Deadline: Late January

Wal-Mart Foundation
Scholarship program
702 S.W. 8th Street
Bentonville, AR 72716-8071
www.walmartfoundation.org

Wal-Mart stores offers a variety of college scholarships. Employees' kids, for
example, can apply for a $6,000 scholarship. This award is based on the stu-
dent's academic record, ACT/SAT scores, and financial need. In addition,
each Wal-Mart store and SAM'S Club awards a $1,000 scholarship to a qual-
ifying local high school senior. More than 2,400 scholarships are given
annually.

Deadline: Varies

Coca-Cola Scholars Foundation
800-306-2653
www.coca-colascholars.org

50 National Scholars receive $20,000 each, and 200 Regional Scholars $4,000,
over a period of four years. Coca-Cola scholarships are awarded based on
character, personal merit and commitment. Merit is demonstrated through
leadership in school, civic and extracurricular activities and academic
achievement.

Deadline: October 31

Educational Communications Scholarship Foundation
www.honoring.com
Contact: Your school guidance office

Through two separate programs, this foundation awards 250 scholarships of
$1,000 each, for a total of $250,000 annually.

Deadline: All students who are listed in Who's Who Among American High
School Students, a publication that honors high-achieving students, will
automatically receive a scholarship application

Elks National Foundation
2750 North Lakeview Avenue
Chicago, IL 60614-1889
773-929-2100
www.elks.org

The Elks National Foundation offers more than $3.3 million in college schol-
arships each year. The Most Valuable Student, Eagle Scout, and Girl Scout
Gold Award scholarships are open to any graduating high school senior. No
Elks affiliation is needed. The Most Valuable Student awards give 500 four-
year scholarships, ranging from $1,000 to $15,000 per year, based on finan-

cial need, leadership, and scholarship. Legacy awards are one-year, merit-based scholarships of $1,000, for children and grandchildren of Elks members.

Deadline: Varies, depending on the type of scholarship

Guideposts' Young Writers Contest
16 East 34th Street
New York, NY 10016
800-251-8169
www.guidepost.com/young_writers_contest.asp

Entrants must write a first-person story about a memorable or moving experience they have had. Stories must be the true personal experience of the writer. Authors of the top 10 manuscripts will each receive a scholarship, ranging from $10,000 (for first prize) to $1,000 (sixth through tenth prize). Those who place eleventh through twentieth will receive $250.

Deadline: Last Monday in November

CHAPTER 9

Smart Borrowing

You socked away money regularly in a college savings fund. Your child has applied for financial aid and scholarships, and he has even been awarded a solid aid package. Yet you are still coming up short.

No one plans on borrowing money to send their kids to college, but chances are even if you have saved steadily over the years, even if your child receives some financial aid, you will still need to borrow some money to get that diploma. Why? Some portion of most financial aid packages is generally a loan (a very low-cost loan, yes, but a loan nonetheless). As we have seen, the cost of a college education is high. Even super-saving families generally cannot save the *entire* amount, and, even if your Expected Family Contribution (EFC) is substantially less than the full price of tuition, that expected cost may still be more than your family can cobble together from savings and current cash flow.

When it comes to loans, student loans are often the best deal around. Student loans, in fact, are probably the best source of college money to go after, says Raymond D. Loewe, a chartered financial consultant and the president of College Money, a college-planning firm in Marlton, New Jersey. Like most other deals, though, some are better than others. The Perkins loan with its 5 percent interest rate is a great deal, and in most cases, you would be crazy to turn down a subsidized Stafford loan because Uncle Sam pays the interest while your child attends school. An unsubsidized Stafford loan is often a good deal, too, because it offers low interest rates and flexible repayment terms, but in some cases, you may simply prefer to borrow the money *privately* (that is, from a source other than the federal government), or you may simply get a better deal if you borrow the money from *yourself*. A home equity line of credit, for instance, can be a good choice.

Some parents do not want their students taking on college loans. They do not want to saddle their children with large loans as they start life after college, says Loewe, but that can be a mistake. "Student loans give children a vested interest in their education. If they know that borrowing money is part of the college cost, they tend to do better," says Loewe. To convince clients that it is okay to expect to kids to take out a reasonable amount of college loans, Loewe asks parents: Who is better off with college loans? Your child, who is just starting out in a career and probably will not retire for decades, or you, with retirement right around the corner?

Fortunately, you do not have to decide this issue right away. In most cases, you do not have to worry about applying for a loan or deciding which type of loan you want until your child has decided which school she wants to attend (from among the schools in which she was accepted) and you know how much money (if any) you have coming to you in terms of financial aid and scholarships. At that point, it is time to decide about loans. Of course, it does not hurt to be prepared. Thinking about the type of loans now that you might use and how much money you can borrow and *would be willing* to borrow may help you ultimately decide which schools you can afford. This chapter will help you understand the

THE TRUE COST OF EDUCATION LOANS

Whether the loans you apply for are funded by the government or a private institution, be sure you understand these basic terms, says USA Funds, the nation's largest guarantor of education loans:

- **The interest rate**   Most education loans have a variable rate and an interest rate cap. Determine if the rate is indexed or linked to a published rate like Treasury bill rates and how often the rate changes. Ask for estimates of what your total interest charges and total indebtedness will be.

- **Fees**   Most loans have origination fees. The federal loan fee goes to the federal government to offset costs. There also may be a guarantee fee, which goes to a guarantor for insuring the loan. These fees are deducted from the principal amount disbursed.

- **In-school payments**   Will you have to make payments while you are in school? Requirements vary for different loan types.

- **Federal interest benefits**   On some loans, the government pays the interest during in-school, grace, and deferment periods.

- **Grace period**   In some cases, there is a grace period after a student leaves school, during which no payment is required.

various types of loans available and the particular terms of those loans, such as interest rates, repayment options, and the amount you can borrow.

Federal Loans

When it comes to borrowing money for college, many students and their parents look to Uncle Sam for assistance. Why? Federal loans often offer the lowest rates in town. In some cases, you do not have to pay any interest on the borrowed funds until the student graduates from college. What is more, repayment terms are rather flexible and, depending on the career that the student pursues and other variables, some loans may even be forgiven.

The Perkins Loan (Formerly, the National Defense Loan Program)

A Perkins loan is cheap, cheap, cheap. Students with exceptional financial need can borrow up to $4,000 per year at a 5-percent interest rate. Aside from interest, there is no additional charge for this loan. Payments can be deferred beyond the customary 10-year period and perhaps even cancelled if the graduate joins the Peace Corps or pursues certain other occupations. The trouble with a Perkins loan, though, is that you cannot apply for it on your own. Federal Perkins loans are granted to lower-income students through a school's financial aid office. *It is part of a financial aid package.* Although the loan is made with government funds (and some money contributed by the school), the school is actually the lender. The school will either write you a check for the loan amount (usually two payments per year), or it will apply the loan amount directly to your school charges.

Repayment

Your child does not have to start repaying a Perkins loan until nine months after she graduates, leaves school, or drops below half-time status as a student. (This nine-month period is called a *grace period*.) An estimated payment for a $15,000 loan would be $150.81 per month, over a 10-year period. In most cases, you have up to 10 years to repay a Perkins loan.

If your child cannot make these payments, she can apply for a loan *deferment.* Deferments are not automatic. The student must apply for one through her school by filling out a deferment request form. What are some conditions that qualify for deferment? Your daughter is attending graduate school at least half-time, or she is unable to find a job. A Perkins loan may be forgiven entirely. That means your daughter does not have to pay the money back at all, if:

- She teaches at a school that serves low-income families.
- She teaches children with disabilities or she teaches math, science, a foreign language, or some other subject that has a shortage of teachers.
- She works as a nurse, medical technician, or law enforcement or corrections officer.

Stafford Loans

These are what most people mean when they talk about student loans. Stafford loans are available to students from all income levels. You can borrow up to $2,625 for the first year of college, $3,500 for the second year, and up to $5,500 for each of the remaining two or three years that it takes to graduate. Generally, the total amount that an undergraduate student can borrow, from all Stafford loans combined, is $23,000. Independent students who live on their own can borrow more, up to $46,000 during their college career. (These amounts are based on enrollment for a full academic year. For part-time students, the maximum loan amount is reduced.)

Depending on the school that your child attends, your Stafford loan will be made through either the Federal Family Education Loan program (FFEL) or the William D. Ford Federal Direct Loan program (Direct Loan). The terms and conditions of both loans are almost identical. Both loans let you borrow the same amount, and the deferment and cancellation provisions are the same. The major differences between the two programs? The source of the funds and certain repayment options. Under the Direct Loan program, for instance, the funds for your loan come directly from the federal government. Funds for your FFEL will come from a bank, credit union, or some other lender that participates in the program. Most FFEL loans must be paid back within 10 years, while you can take up to 30 years to repay a Direct Loan.

Obviously, you will have to pay interest on these loans. The rate is variable and can change each year of repayment. (Rates are set each June at 3.1 points over the three-month Treasury Bill.) However, these rates are capped: By law, the interest rate will never exceed 8.25 percent. In addition, you will have to pay a fee of up to 4 percent of the loan. (Typically, there is a 3 percent loan origination fee and a 1 percent guarantee fee.) This fee is deducted proportionately from each loan disbursement.

Subsidized versus Unsubsidized

Although you do not have to make any loan payments until after graduation, interest begins accruing on these loans as soon as you receive the money. When you will have to start paying that interest, though, depends again on the type of loan you get. Direct and FFEL Stafford loans come in subsidized and unsubsidized versions. A *subsidized* loan is given based on financial need. (Again, you cannot apply for this directly. A subsidized loan is awarded as part of a financial aid package.) Your child does not have to pay the interest on this loan while he is still in school. That is why it is called a subsidized loan because the government subsidizes the interest for you during the college years. An *unsubsidized* loan, however, is not need-based. These loans are available to all students. Interest starts accruing as soon as you receive the loaned funds. You can pay the interest now or let the interest accumulate (until the student graduates).

If you let the interest accumulate, it will be capitalized. That is, the interest will be added to the principal amount of your loan so, ultimately, you will owe a higher principal.

Repayment

Your child does not have to start repaying a *subsidized* Stafford loan (that is, the Direct Stafford or the FFEL Stafford) until six months (grace period) after he graduates, leaves school, or drops below half-time status as a student. Repayments are usually due monthly. An estimated monthly payment on a $15,000 loan, for example, is $184.00 per month. Generally, you can choose the standard 10-year repayment plan or one of the other extended repayment plans. (see the following sidebar).

With an *unsubsidized* Stafford loan, however, the rules are a bit different. The student still has until six months after graduation to begin repayment of principal, but interest charges are due immediately. Your child can pay the interest while he attends college. That is difficult for most students, though, unless you are giving your child the money, or he can defer the interest payments until he graduates and begins making the loan repayments. (In the long run, this will cost more, obviously.)

Like the Perkins loan, however, your child may be able to postpone payment of the loan after graduation—for up to three years—if she is attending graduate school at least half-time or unable to find a full-time job. However, only the principal is deferred with an unsubsidized Stafford loan. Interest payments are still due. (No interest payments are due, during a deferment, with a subsidized Stafford.) Stafford loans can be canceled entirely under a few rare circumstances such as bankruptcy or death. However, Stafford loans *cannot* be canceled because:

- Your son did not complete his program of study (unless the school closed and he was unable to finish it).
- Your son did not like the school or the program of study.
- Your son could not find a job.

Parent Loans for Undergraduate Students (PLUS)

As its name implies, this is a loan for parents. You borrow the money on your child's behalf, and as you might expect, you are responsible for paying Uncle Sam back. This loan can be repaid over a 10-year period.

With a PLUS loan, you do not need to satisfy a need test. Any parent, rich, poor, or in the middle, can apply for this loan. You will need to satisfy a credit check by the lender. However, the credit standards for this loan are reportedly less stringent than credit standards for a mortgage, for example, or other non-federally guaranteed loans. If you do not pass the credit check, you may still be able to receive a loan if someone, such as a relative or friend who *is* able to pass the credit check, agrees to endorse the loan.

A PLUS has a variable interest rate that can change each year. (The federal government put it at 3.1 percent above the 12-month U.S. Treasury Bill.) However, the PLUS's interest rate will never exceed 9 percent. In addition, the PLUS charges a 1 percent guarantee fee and a 3 percent origination fee (like the Stafford). Want some more good news? There is no limit as to how much you can borrow. In some cases, you can finance the entire cost of your child's education, including tuition, living expenses, and books, less any financial aid received.

Like Stafford loans, PLUS loans are available through both the Direct Loan and FFEL programs. With a Direct PLUS loan, the U.S. Department of Education will send the loan funds directly to your child's school. With a FFEL PLUS loan, the loan funds will be sent your child's school by the lender. (In this case, the lender could be a bank, a credit union, or another type of private lender.)

How do you apply? The processes are a bit different for the Direct Plus and the FFEL Plus. With a both types of loans, you must fill out a Direct PLUS Loan Application and Promissory Note, which is available from your school's financial aid office. Because it is not financial aid, you do not have to fill out a Free Application for Federal Student Aid (FAFSA), though, unless the college requires you to do so. (More colleges, it seems, are making such requests of parents.)

With a Direct Plus, the lender is the U.S. Department of Education. The school works directly with the Department of Education to process the loan and disburse the money. (You do not have to do anything.) With a FFEL Plus loan, however, you must find a lender. The school may help you do this. If not, contact the guaranty agency that serves your state. (For your state agency's telephone number, see the list of state agencies at the end of Chapter 6.)

Repayment

PLUS loans, unfortunately, have no grace periods. Monthly repayments generally start 60 days after your borrow the money. Unlike the Stafford loan, you must begin repaying both principal and interest immediately, while your child is still in college. Generally, you can choose the standard 10-year repayment plan or one of the other extended repayment plans. (see the following sidebar). With a FFEL PLUS loan, however, the lender will arrange the repayment schedule. Typically, most lenders ask that you pay at least $600 per year, so that your loan is paid off in no longer than 10 years.

In some cases, however, you may be able to defer payment for up to three years. Under what circumstances? Eligibility rules for requesting a deferment for PLUS loans are the same as those for Stafford loans. However, because all PLUS loans are unsubsidized, only the principal can be deferred. You will still be charged interest during deferment periods. PLUS loans can be canceled entirely under a few rare circumstances (such as bankruptcy or death). However, PLUS loans *cannot* be canceled because:

- Your son did not complete his program of study (unless the school closed and he was unable to finish it).
- Your son did not like the school or the program of study.
- Your son could not find a job.

Repayment Schedules

There are several different repayment options for these types of loans. Direct Stafford borrowers can pick a repayment schedule from among the first four options outlined in the following. FFEL Stafford borrowers, however, have just three options: standard, graduated, and income-sensitive. Direct Plus borrowers cannot use the income contingent or income-sensitive options. You can pick a different repayment plan once a year, but if you do not pick any of the options initially, you will automatically repay under the standard repayment plan. To make payment easier, you can also consolidate all of your federal loans into one loan so you will have one monthly payment. (See the previous sidebar on consolidation for other benefits of consolidating federal loans.)

Which option is better? Obviously, it depends on your individual circumstances, but bear in mind that the longer you take to repay your loan in full, the more money you may ultimately pay in interest. Monthly payments under the extended plan will likely be less than monthly payments under the standard plan for the same loan amount. Over the life of the loan, though, you will pay the exact same amount in principal, but more in interest for the extended loan because you are borrowing the money for a longer period of time:

- **The standard repayment plan** You pay a fixed amount each month, at least $50, for up to 10 years. Generally, this is the quickest and least expensive way to pay back a student loan.
- **The graduated repayment plan** Your payments will be lower at first and then increase over time (generally every two years). The logic here? A student's financial situation is expected to improve gradually, as he advances in his career or profession. The length of your repayment period will range from 12 to 30 years, depending on your loan amount.
- **The extended repayment plan** You can stretch your payments for a longer time period, up to 30 years, depending on the loan amount. Your payments can be fixed or graduated (lower at first and then increased over time).

(continued)

Repayment Schedules (*continued*)

- **The income contingent repayment plan** Your monthly payment is based on your yearly income, family size, and loan amount. As your income rises or falls, so do your loan payments. If you have a low income, you can make just minimum payments. (Payments can be so low, in fact, that they may not even cover the cost of interest.) After 25 years, any remaining balance on the loan may be forgiven. You may have to pay taxes on the forgiven amount, however, which could be considerable. If you do not have the money to pay the money, you may not have the money to pay the taxes due either, so this debt could just go on and on.

- **The income-sensitive plan** Your monthly payment is based on your yearly income and your loan amount. Like the income contingent plan, your payments rise, or fall, with your income. The difference: Your monthly payments must at least cover the cost of interest.

Consolidate Your Loans

To simplify payment, you can consolidate all of your federal college loans, that includes most federal student loans and PLUS loans, into one loan. You can even consolidate just one loan into a direct consolidation loan to get more flexible repayment options. (For example, your current loan may not have an income-sensitive repayment option.) If you have more than one loan, a consolidation loan simplifies the repayment process: You make just one payment per month. In addition, the interest rate on a consolidation loan may be lower than the rate on your other loans. Both the Direct Loan program and the FFEL program offer consolidation loans. Direct consolidation loans are available from the U.S. Department of Education. FFEL consolidation loans are available from participating lenders such as banks, credit unions, and savings and loan associations.

The interest rate for consolidation loans is fixed for the length of the loan and cannot exceed 8.25 percent. You can get a consolidate loan during your grace period (that is, before you actually start making loan repayments) or once you have started making repayments. However, consolidation can cost you a lot more in interest if your payments are stretched out over a longer period of time. Before consolidating, make sure that you understand all of the terms of the new loan and how much it is going to cost in the long run.

FORBEARANCE

If students do not qualify for a deferment, but cannot make their loan payments, they may qualify for a *forbearance*. During a forbearance, you do not have to make interest or premium payments, even if you have an unsubsidized Stafford loan. However, interest will accrue during this period on both unsubsidized and subsidized loans. Forbearance may last for up to three years, but you must reapply for forbearance every year (and you must supply documentation that the forbearance is necessary). Forbearance may be granted, for example, if the borrower (in this case, the parent or the student) cannot make payments due to poor health or other unseen personal problems. An automatic forbearance is granted if loan payments are at least 20 percent of the borrower's monthly gross income. (However, you must still apply for this forbearance.)

THE STUDENT LOAN INTEREST DEDUCTION

Thanks to current changes in the tax law, the cost of borrowing for college has gotten somewhat cheaper. (Well, for some parents anyway.) Here is how it works: Taxpayers can deduct the interest paid on qualified education loans up to $2,500 annually.

To qualify for this deduction, the student must be enrolled at least half-time in a college or university, or some other degree-granting or certification program. The deduction can be claimed by whoever takes out the loan, either you (the parent) or your child (the student), and most types of loans qualify. In other words, it does not have to be a federal Stafford loan. A home equity loan would not qualify, however, because the interest on those loans is already tax deductible.

Like most other federal tax deductions, there are income-eligibility limitations on these student loan interest deductions. The income limits for married taxpayers filing joint returns have been raised to $100,000 to $130,000 and for single taxpayers to $50,000 to $65,000. In addition, married taxpayers filing separate returns do not qualify, no matter what their income, and no deduction is allowed for anyone who is claimed as a dependent on another person's tax return. (That means your son cannot take this deduction if you are still claiming him as a dependent on your tax return.)

State Loans

You will also find some student loans available through your state. Some of these are state specific. That is, they are only available through a particular state. Minnesota, for instance, offers the Student Educational Loan Fund (SELF) program. This program is unique to Minnesota, and the Minnesota Higher Education Services Office is the program's only lender. However, the money is available to residents who attend in-state *or* out-of-state colleges as well as to non-residents who attend a college in Minnesota.

Private, or Alternative, Loans

Uncle Sam is not the only borrowing source in town. Several not-for-profit organizations, such as TERI and Sallie Mae, offer private, or *alternative,* loans, at rates slightly higher than government-sponsored Stafford and PLUS loans, to students who did not apply for federal loans, did not qualify for federal loans, or who need additional funds.

The Education Resources Institute (TERI)

TERI's Alternative loan lets you (or your child) borrow up to the cost of your child's education (less financial aid received). The interest charged is prime plus zero, and there is a 5 to 6.5 percent origination fee, depending on the repayment schedule. You can select from a list of national lenders: Bank of America, BankOne, Charter One Bank, FSB, Citizens Bank, First Union National Bank/Educaid, Fleet, National City, and PNC. To qualify, students must be enrolled in school at least half time, and they must meet certain credit guidelines, such as a satisfactory two-year credit history and sufficient current income. In most cases, that means that parents must co-sign.

If your child is attending school less than full time, you (or your child) can apply for a TERI Continuing Education Loan (CEL). You can borrow from $500 up to $15,000, annually. Like the Alternative loan, approval is based on credit-worthiness, which often means that parents must co-sign. This loan costs a bit more than the Alternative: The rate is prime plus 0 to 1.5 percent, depending on the borrower selected. Again, you must pay an origination fee of 5 percent, and you can borrow from national lenders such as Charter One Bank, FSB, Citizens Bank, Fleet, and National City. For more information or to apply for a loan, contact TERI at 800-255-8374, *www.teri.org.*

REPAYMENT

With TERI's Alternative loan, you can repay your loan (that is, principal and interest) immediately. Well, almost immediately. Monthly payments begin 30 days after the funds are disbursed. This is option one and obviously, this will cost you the least amount in interest. A second option lets you pay just interest while the student is enrolled in college. You can defer payment of principal until six months after your child graduates or leaves school. A third option lets you defer the whole payment, that is, interest and principal, until your child graduates or leaves college. Over the long term, however, the difference in price among these three different payment options can be surprisingly significant. Let us say that you borrow $20,000, which you then repay over a 20-year period at 9 percent interest. With option one, that loan (with interest) will ultimately cost you $48,149.78. Option two will cost you $56,148.03. Option three costs $75,549.71. That is more than three times the amount of the original loan!

Let us look at this a little bit closer. The reason that option three costs so much is because you are deferring all payment until the child gets out of school. That may seem like a great idea at the time, and in some cases, especially if the student is actually borrowing the money, you may not have any other options. Okay. If you are really strapped for cash now, you must resign yourself to paying scads of interest, end of story. However, most other folks should really do the math before buying into this deferment deal.

Using our previous example, you would have to make monthly payments of $166.63, while your child is still in college, to change option three to option two. If you defer full payment until after college, your monthly payments will rise to about $275. Could you swing those payments earlier? Yes? Then think about paying the principal, too (that is option one). It would cost just another $30 per month—yes, $30—and look at all the money you would save in interest. The point is: Making principal and interest payments now, rather than deferring them, might not break your current budget as much as you think, and making interest-only payments just does not do all that much to fill your pockets today. In this case, it is just $30. Many people spend that amount without thinking, yet added to your monthly loan payment, it will save you thousands in interest. Obviously, the difference between your loan repayment of interest-only and a loan repayment of principal and interest will probably be higher because we are only talking about a $10,000 loan in this case. Still, you have to do the math. Is the lower payment really going to ease your cash flow? Or could you squeeze some extra dollars out of your current budget and, thereby, save a significant amount of money over the life of the loan?

With TERI's CEL, repayment of principal and interest begins six months after disbursement. You cannot defer payment until after graduation.

Sallie Mae

Sallie Mae partners with a nationwide network of lenders, such as Bank of America, Coastal Federal Credit Union, and Bank One, to offer the Signature Education Loan program. Part of this package includes Federal Stafford loans, which were discussed in the federal loan section previously. If you need or want funding beyond the limits of the federal program, however, Sallie Mae also offers its own Signature loan. You can borrow up to $100,000. Interest rates are variable and are determined, in part, by your credit rating. A borrower with an excellent credit rating, for example, would qualify for an interest rate of prime plus 0.5 percent. A borrower with only a fair rating, however, would pay prime plus 2 percent. These rates can be lowered, though, if a parent (with a stronger credit history, presumably) co-signs the loan.

A neat perk with these loans? You can apply simultaneously for a Stafford loan and a Signature loan through Sallie Mae. That means, you will receive one monthly billing statement, and have to make one monthly payment as a result, for all of these loans. Generally, such payments are easier and more convenient to budget. For more information, contact Sallie Mae at 800-222-7182 or *www .salliemae.com*.

REPAYMENT

Payments begin six months after graduation, or if the student drops out of school, or attends school less than half time. Sallie Mae offers a variety of repayment options. With a standard repayment account, you pay both principal and interest each month throughout your loan repayment term. Obviously, you will pay the least amount of total interest using this arrangement.

A graduated repayment account, however, lets you make interest-only payments during the first few years so that your payments are more affordable. Afterward, you make larger repayments of principal and interest, so that you still repay the entire loan in the standard 10-year time frame. The Flex Repay Account, Sallie Mae's newest graduated repayment plan, lets you pay interest-only payments initially. (These early payments can be more than 40 percent lower than the payments you would make under the standard payment plan.) In addition, you can extend the total loan repayment for another five years. That all sounds terrific, of course, but remember: Nobody lends you money for free.

The longer you take to pay the money back, that includes making those interest-only payments to make your monthly payments more manageable, the more it will cost you, in the long run, in interest. Because you are not paying the principal down as quickly, you will pay more interest over the life of the loan.

Nellie Mae

Nellie Mae offers both federal and private loans for parents and students. Federal loans available through Nellie Mae include Stafford loans, PLUS loans, and a federal consolidation loan. For college students, Nellie Mae offers its own loan, called the EXCEL education loan. There is an EXCEL for parents and another one for students.

Unlike the Federal PLUS loan that is restricted to parents only, EXCEL loans are available to any creditworthy individual (that is, a parent, spouse, another relative, or a friend) who is willing to borrow money on behalf of your child. This EXCEL loan lets you borrow from $500 up to the total cost of attendance (less other financial aid received). You have two interest rate options. The annual variable rate, which is set on August 1 for the upcoming school year, is prime plus 2 percent. The monthly variable is prime plus 0.75 percent, and it is adjusted (if necessary) at the beginning of each month. In addition, you do not pay an origination fee with an EXCEL, but you do pay a 7 percent guarantee fee. (This fee is put in an insurance fund that protects the lender against any loan default.) To qualify, you must be creditworthy and your debt payments—that includes credit card balances, your monthly mortgage payments, *and* the payments on the EXCEL loan itself—cannot exceed 40 percent of your gross income.

Students can borrow up to $10,000 on their own, or if a creditworthy parent co-signs, up to the cost of attendance, less any financial aid received. All freshman borrowers need a co-signer. In subsequent years, however, it is possible that the student's creditworthiness will be sufficient. Students pay a 6 percent guarantee fee, or if they have a co-signer, just a 2 percent guarantee fee. Like the parent version of this loan, the student borrower has the same two interest rate options. The only difference? The monthly rate is lower: It is prime plus 0 percent. You can only use the student version at Nellie Mae-eligible colleges. Most schools are eligible, but it is wise to check just to be sure. (Contact Nellie Mae at 800-634-9308 or *www.nelliemae.com* to find out if your child's school is eligible.)

REPAYMENT

With the parent's EXCEL loan, you can pay principal and interest immediately, within 45 days of the first disbursement. Or you can make interest-only payments while your child is attending college. You have up to 20 years to repay the loan, depending on the amount borrowed. (Again, the longer you take to repay the loan, the more it will cost you, ultimately, in interest.)

Depending on how much you borrow, you have up to 20 years to repay the student EXCEL loan, too, after graduation. No payments are required while the student is in school at least half time.

P.L.A.T.O.

P.L.A.T.O. is the University Support Service's loan program. Like Sallie Mae and Nellie Mae, P.L.A.T.O. can hook you up with federal Stafford loans, but it also offers its own loan, the Classic Student loan. Students can borrow from $1,000 to $20,000 per year (up to a maximum of $80,000 total). That money can be used to finance all of your education-related expenses, such as tuition, room and board, even a personal computer. Interest rates are variable: It is prime plus a spread of 0 percent to 10 percent. How much spread you will pay depends on your credit rating. Like Sallie Mae and Nellie Mae, students without an established credit history may need Mom or Dad to co-sign.

REPAYMENT

You have 15 years to repay a P.L.A.T.O. loan. You can make principal and interest payments right away. Or, like most other student loans, you can defer paying principal until six months after graduation. For more information, contact P.L.A.T.O. at 800-467-5286 or *www.plato.org*.

Borrow from Yourself

Stafford loans, PLUS loans, and many of the private education loans are often great deals, but you probably have another, cheap borrowing source at your fingertips, too. If you own a home, have a life insurance policy or a retirement account, you can borrow from *yourself*. That is, you can borrow from or against your house or other assets to pay your child's tuition bills.

Borrowing against Your Home

If you own a home, you may be able to borrow against the equity in your house to pay for college. This kind of borrowing is especially attractive because the interest rate is generally low. Typically, it is slightly more than prime. (At this writing, the prime rate is a remarkably low 4.25 percent.) Unlike other consumer loans, the interest paid on this loan up to $100,000 is tax-deductible.

In most cases, you can borrow up to 80 percent of your home's equity. (That is your home's current value minus what you owe on your mortgage.) If your house is worth $250,000, for example, and you owe $100,000 on your mortgage, you have $150,000 in equity in your house. That means you can probably borrow up to 80 percent of $150,000, or $120,000.

Home equity borrowing comes in two basic types: the home equity loan and the home equity line of credit. The *home equity loan* works much like your first mortgage. (In fact, it is often referred to as a second mortgage.) You borrow a fixed amount of money, which you receive in a lump sum. You repay the loan in monthly installments over a fixed period, generally 10 or 15 years. The interest rate can be fixed or variable. You have to pay points and closing costs, just like you did when you got that first mortgage.

The trouble with a home equity loan, though, is that you must take all of the needed money out in advance. That means, you would have to estimate, at the end of your child's senior year of high school most likely, how much four years at the university is going to cost. Many people find it difficult to make such long-term estimates. However, if you are the type of person who likes to know what you are up against in advance, in terms of interest owed and other terms of the loan, so that you can think ahead about how you will meet those payments, then this type of loan might actually work best for you.

In addition, you must pay interest on the entire amount from the very first day that you take out the loan. Perhaps more importantly, though, you will suddenly have this stockpile of cash that you will not be fully depleting until four years from now. One-fourth of those funds may go to the school directly, but what about the other three-fourths? This cash must now be managed over the next few years so that you can tap into it when you need to make tuition payments. That is not the difficult part, though. You could probably just plunk it into a separate money market account (or invest it in some other short-term safe investment) and write checks directly from the account. The trouble, says Raymond Loewe, is that this cash could have a negative effect on financial aid. Home equity does not appear as an asset for financial aid (if the school uses the FAFSA form). However, in this case, you are pulling cash out of an asset that does not count and turning it into a cash asset that does count. (If the school uses the Profile or its own financial aid form, it probably will not matter because the equity in your home is counted, whether you tap into that equity and convert it to cash or not. See Chapter 7 for an explanation of how the different financial aid forms count assets.)

A *home equity line of credit* works like a revolving credit line typical of most major credit cards. At the outset, you are approved for a certain amount of money. As an example, let us say you are approved for $80,000. For the next 5 or 10 years (depending on the terms of the loan agreement), you can draw on that credit line, in full or in part, whenever you want, and pay interest only on the amount actually drawn. You could withdraw that $80,000 all at once. (However, for college payment purposes, you would not need to.) Or, and this is the likely scenario, you would withdraw the money as you need it. This semester, you withdraw $7,000 to pay for tuition, for example, and perhaps another $500 for books and supplies.

Your monthly payments, as a result, would be a percentage (about 2 percent) of the outstanding balance of the line. (That is the amount you have actually withdrawn, not the amount you can ultimately withdraw.) Typically, you can make these payments and keep making additional withdrawals until you have reached your approved limit over the next 10 or 15 years. Then, depending on the terms of the loan agreement, you may have another 10 years to pay all of the borrowed funds back. (During this repayment period, you cannot withdraw any more money.)

Unfortunately, a home equity line of credit can get quite expensive if you stretch the payments out too long. Extend the payments over years and years, for example, and you run the same risks that you do with a credit card: You will rack up hefty interest payments. Instead, try to repay the full amount within four or five years of your child's graduation. That should keep interest payments to a reasonable level. You will have to compare the terms, of course, but anything longer and you will probably pay less interest with another type of loan.

The downside to both types of home equity borrowing? You are using your house as collateral for the loan. If you default on the payments over an extended period of time, the bank can then take your house as payment.

Refinancing Your Home Mortgage

Instead of taking out a home equity loan, you can tap into your home's equity in another way: Refinance your mortgage. A cash-out refinance lets you trade in your current mortgage for a larger one and pocket the extra money to pay for Suzie's college tuition. However, this is a time-consuming process. (Often, it takes as long as obtaining a first mortgage does.) In most cases, you must pay closing costs of $500 to $5,000. Generally, this is not a good source of funding unless you were planning on refinancing anyway to take advantage of lower mortgage interest rates.

Loans against a Life Insurance Policy

You can borrow up to 90 percent of your whole life or universal life policy's cash value. (Term insurance does not have a cash value, though, so you cannot borrow against it.) You do not need to pay the loan back, ever. The loan (plus interest) will simply be subtracted from the face value of the policy that is paid to your beneficiaries when you die.

For many folks, it is easy to borrow money this way. All you have to do is call your insurance agent. There are no applications or credit checks, and in many cases, you will receive a check within days. If you have not held the policy very long, however, you will not be able to borrow against it. Commissions and start-up costs consume most of your early premiums. Cash does not really start accumulating in a policy until year four or so. In addition, calculating the actual cost of this loan is not as easy as it seems (no matter what your insurance agent says).

Here is how it works: When you borrow against your life insurance policy, you are borrowing against the policy's cash value. The good news is that your cash value will continue to earn interest, even the portion that you borrow against it. The bad news, however, is that in many cases, your cash value will earn interest at a lower rate than it did before.

Let us say that your policy now earns 8 percent interest. If you borrow money from the policy, the interest rate may be cut to 6 percent, let us say, on the portion of the cash value that you have borrowed against. That is a good deal, your insurance agent may argue. It is only costing you 2 percent to borrow the money. (His math: 8 percent − 6 percent = 2 percent.) Where else can you get a deal like that? No place. In fact, you are not really getting that rate in this situation either.

If you were earning 8 percent, but are now earning 6 percent, than it is indeed costing you 2 percent. However, that is not the whole cost! You have to pay interest on the money you borrow, too. It may seem like you are *not* paying interest because the money is deducted from the policy's cash value and you are not actually writing a check for it. In one way or another, you are paying interest. To find the trust cost, then, you have to add in the interest charge. Let us say that your interest rate is 7 percent. In this case, the true cost of a loan against your policy is not the 2 percent your insurance advisor suggested, but 9 percent. That is the 2 percent rate of return that you lost to borrow the money, plus the 7 percent interest rate.

If you do not plan on paying this type of loan back, you will have to think about how this change could ultimately affect your family. Typically, life insurance is bought as protection for your family. That is especially true if you plan to pay all or part of your child's tuition out of your current income. If you die while your son is still in college, for example, the death benefit of that insurance policy should cover your future lost income (depending on the amount and terms of your policy) and not affect your family's ability to pay those college bills. Should you take out a loan and die before it is paid back, however, your family may have to scramble to find other means of financing your son's education. In an extreme situation, your son may not be able to afford to stay in school.

Loans from Retirement Plans

If you have been steadily socking away money into your retirement fund throughout your working years, you probably have accumulated a tidy nest egg by this point. As you probably already know, many retirement plans let you borrow money from your account and pay the money back, with interest, of course, to your own account. Why not tap into those funds, then, to help pay for college?

The answer, of course, is never that simple. First, although many retirement plans do enable you to borrow from your account, not all do. Most defined-contribution plans, such as a 401(k) or its sister plan, a 403(b) that is offered to teachers, hospital workers, and other non-profit workers, for example, let you borrow from your account. Traditional pension plans, or defined benefit plans, that promise to pay a defined benefit at retirement, for example, do not permit borrowing of any kind. Nor can you borrow from IRAs or IRA based plans such as SEP-IRAs.

Secondly, the savings advantage is not always as favorable as it appears. If you borrow money from your retirement fund, you can generally borrow up to 50 percent of your account's assets, up to $50,000. Because you are essentially borrowing your own money, you then pay this money back (with interest) into your own account (rather than to a bank or lender). At first glance, this seems like a free loan. You are borrowing your own money, and you are paying yourself the interest!

It is not quite that simple, of course. Let us look at an example. You have borrowed $25,000 from your 401(k). Before you took the money out of the account, it was invested in a stock mutual fund that was earning 10 percent. Now, however, you have borrowed the money so it is no longer earning the 10 percent. Instead, it is earning 6 percent. That is the interest you are paying on the borrowed amount, and you are paying that interest into your account. So, the loan is a bargain because it is only costing you 4 percent, right? (The math: 10 percent − 10 percent.)

Wrong. This loan is costing you more. Let us look at those numbers again. You are indeed losing the 4 percent. That is the difference between what you were earning on the money previously and the amount of interest you are currently paying. However, you are also losing the 6 percent, even though you are paying the money into your account. Why? You are paying that money out of pocket. In other words, you are using current income to get that 6 percent return. Before you borrowed the money, however, the fund was earning that 10 percent all by itself. You did not put the 10 percent into the account; the money was *growing* by 10 percent. That means, the real cost of the loan is 10 percent because that is what you are losing in investment earnings when you take the funds out.

One real advantage to a retirement account loan is that you can get the money quickly. Often, you can tap into your 401(k) account simply by calling your company's benefits office or the 800 number listed in your plan's informational packet.

If your plan enables loans by phone, you will get a check within a few days. Even if you must fill out a form to request a loan, though, a check should arrive within two weeks. Because you are borrowing your own money, a credit check is not required, and payments are usually deducted directly from your paycheck.

Typically, you must pay this loan back within five years. (A loan taken to buy a home, however, usually can be paid back over a longer time period, often up to 30 years.) Depending on your financial situation, that five-year pay-back feature could work to your advantage. If you are the type to stretch payments over years and years, you will be forced to pay this loan off in five years. Think of all the interest you will save!

If you do not pay the money back within that time frame, however, the loan will be considered a withdrawal. As a result, you will owe regular income taxes plus a 10 percent penalty on the borrowed amount. Another serious drawback: If you quit your job or get fired, you may have to pay the money back, in full, within 60 days, or face the same penalty and tax consequences.

Borrowing against Stocks and Bonds

You can take out a margin loan against your stocks and bonds. How much you can borrow depends on the limits set by your brokerage firm and how much equity you have in your margin account. For instance, you can generally borrow up to 50 percent of the value of certain stocks, up to 85 percent of municipal bonds, and up to 90 percent of U.S. Treasuries. Getting a margin loan is quick, too. Unlike home equity loans, there are no closing costs, no present repayment schedules, and no lengthy applications to complete. (In some cases, the interest rate, which is tied to the broker's call rate, can be lower than the rate for a home equity loan, too.) However, there is always the possibility of a *margin call*, and that makes many people shy away from this loan option. If the market suddenly drops (and your stocks take a beating), you may have to repay all or part of the loan (in cash or with additional securities) within a few days. If you cannot come up with the cash that fast? You will have to sell your stock.

However, that is just the worst case scenario that everyone talks about. Could it happen? Of course, but it is really only likely to happen if you borrow up to the limits of your account. If you limit your borrowing on margin, however, to a small percentage of your account, no more that 25 percent in most cases, then you will probably have very little risk of getting a margin call because you still have the remaining three-fourths of your account (which you have not borrowed against) to cover you.

If you possess a considerable stock and bond portfolio, at this point, you might well be asking: "Isn't it easier to simply sell the stocks and use the cash to pay my son's tuition bills?" It may be easier, but it is not necessarily smarter *financially*. Here is why: When you sell an appreciable asset (such as stocks) you incur *capital gains.* Not only do you have to pay tax on those gains but the gains increase your taxable income for that particular year. That could reduce your chances of getting financial aid.

Personal Loans

You can always consider just borrowing money from a bank. However, the interest paid on an unsecured loan, which is based on your salary, is generally much higher than the interest paid on a loan that is secured with some collateral, such as your home or stocks and bonds. The most expensive kind of personal loan is a cash advance on your credit card. It is not an option for financing college costs, except maybe to buy books if you are temporarily strapped for cash.

Glossary

Asset Protection Allowance   The portion of the parents' assets that is not included in the calculation of the parents' contribution, using the Federal Methodology.

Baccalaureate Bond   A type of municipal bond sold by some states especially for college savings.

Bond   Commonly referred to as a fixed income investment, a bond typically pays an interest income to bondholders on a regular, or fixed, basis.

Certificates of Deposit (CDs)   You deposit a set amount of money—often at a bank—and you are guaranteed a stated interest rate at the end of the period.

CollegeSure CD   A special CD, offered by the College Savings Bank of Princeton, that is designed specifically for college savings.

Coverdell Education Savings Accounts   Formerly known as Education IRAs, these accounts let parents save up to $2,000 per year for college, per child. Withdrawals are not subject to federal income tax. The money saved in an Education Savings Account must generally be used by the time the student reaches age 30.

Delinquency   Failure to make a scheduled loan payment.

Expected Family Contribution (EFC)   The dollar amount that you are expected to pay for college, based on your family's income and assets.

Federal Methodology The formula that the federal government uses to calculate your family's financial need, which determines your eligibility for federal and state financial aid.

Federal Supplemental Educational Opportunity Grant (FSEOG) A federal grant that awards additional need-based money to supplement the Pell Grant.

Financial Need The difference between the student's educational costs and the expected family contribution.

Free Application for Federal Student Aid (FAFSA) The form you must fill out to get federal and state financial aid as well as grants and loans.

Grant Money for college that does not have to be repaid. Grants are usually awarded on the basis of need.

Hope Scholarship Credit Parents can take this tax credit, of up to $1,500 each year, for each student in the family.

Institutional Methodology A formula used by many private schools to determine financial need. Institutional funds are doled out based on this methodology.

Lifetime Learning Credit This 20 percent tax credit of the first $5,000 of qualified college expenses (up to a maximum of $1,000) can be taken during a student's junior and senior years of college.

Mutual Fund A mutual fund lets you pool your money with other investors—under the guidance of a professional money manager—enabling you to invest in a greater variety of stocks, bonds, or other securities.

Pell Grant The largest federal program, the Pell Grant gave students in the year 2001 a maximum of $3,300 per year.

Perkins Loan Students with extreme financial need can borrow up to $4,000 per year for college at a 5 percent interest rate.

PLUS Loans These federal loans enable parents to borrow money for their children's college education.

Prepaid Tuition Plan These state plans enable parents to pay for future college expenses at today's prices.

Profile A financial aid application used by some private colleges and universities to determine eligibility for financial aid.

Risk The danger of losing money invested in a stock, bond, or other type of investment.

ROTC The Reserve Officers Training Corps program is a scholarship program in which the military cover the cost of tuition and other fees in return for military service.

Scholarships   Monetary awards given to students who are gifted in academics, athletics, or the arts. Some scholarships are based on merit alone; others are based on merit and need.

Stafford Loans   Generally, what people mean when they talk about student loans. There are two varieties: subsidized Stafford loans and unsubsidized Stafford loans.

State-Sponsored Tuition Savings Plans   Called 529s because of the section of the U.S. Tax Code that governs them, these plans enable people to save money, tax-deferred, for college. Under the current tax law, withdrawals are exempt from federal taxes.

Stock   A share of stock represents partial ownership of a company. This type of investment offers great potential gains—and great potential risks.

Student Aid Report   The official notification sent to students after submitting the FAFSA form.

Subsidized Stafford Loan   Interest starts accruing on this loan as soon as the funds are disbursed. You can pay the interest immediately or let it accumulate until the student graduates from college.

Unsubsidized Stafford Loan   You do not have to pay interest on this loan while the student is still in college.

Work Study Programs   A type of financial aid whereby students work at an on- or off-campus job to earn money to pay for college.

Index

allocating investments and portfolio
    management, 31–35
    child's name vs. your name in, 36–42
    college (ages 19 to 22), 34
    elementary (ages 5 to 9), 33
    529 tuition savings plans and, 50
    high school (ages 14 to 18), 34
    middle school (ages 10 to 13), 33
    picking stocks, bonds, mutual funds for,
        35–43
    prepaid tuition programs and, 61
    pre-school (ages 0 to 4), 32–33
    timing in, 32
alternative loans, 105, 168–172
asset protection allowance, 39
athletic scholarships, 147–149

baccalaureate bonds, 21
bonds, 18–21, 27, 93, 177–178
books and supplies, 5
borrowing (see loans)
building a college fund, 29–43
business risk, 31
Byrd Program, 106

calls (defaults), bond, 19
capital gains, 17, 134, 178
certificates of deposit (CDs), 22–23, 27, 35,
    93
certified financial planners (CFP), 95
certified public accountants (CPA), 98
CollegeSure CD, 22–23
commission-based financial planners,
    96–97
company risk, 31

contribution limits, prepaid tuition
    programs and, 62–63
control of funds
    529 tuition savings plans and, 49
    investing in child's name and, 37–42
    prepaid tuition programs and, 51–52
    Uniform Gifts to Minors Act (UGMA),
        115–116
corporate bonds, 20, 35
cost of college education, 1–13, 111–114
coupon rate, bond, 21
Coverdell (see Education Savings
    Accounts)
credits, tax, 107–111
creditworthiness ratings, bond, 20, 21

deductions, tax, 107–111
defaults, bond, 18–19
Direct Loan program, 162–163
dividends, 17

Economic Growth and Tax Relief and
    Reconciliation Act of 2001, 109
education IRAs (see Education Savings
    Accounts)
Education Savings Accounts (ESAs), 42–43,
    45
Educational Needs Trust, 117
elementary (ages 5 to 9), allocating
    investments for, 33
eligibility for aid, 124–129, 132–136
estimating financial aid, 128
EXCEL education loan, Nellie Mae,
    171–172
expected family contribution (EFC), 3–4, 9,
    124, 125–128, 143, 159

Federal Family Education Loan (FFEL) program, 162–163
federal loans, 161–162
Federal Supplemental Educational Opportunity Grant (FSEOG), 104–105
federal vs. institutional methodology, in financial aid, 106–107, 124
fee-based financial planners, 97
fee-only financial planners, 96
fees, financial planners and, 96, 99
FFEL (see Federal Family Education Loans)
FFEL PLUS loans, 164–168
financial aid gap, 126, 143
financial aid officers, 137
financial need, 124
financial planners, 93–99
Financial Planning Association (FPA), 94, 98
529 plans (see savings plans and 529 plans)
fixed income investments (see bonds)
401K, 21, 134, 176–177
Free Application for Federal Student Aid (FAFSA), 104, 105, 124–125, 128–130, 164
Fund Finder, 143

gift aid (grants), 104–105
gifts, 38, 112, 115–117
global mutual funds, 25, 35
government securities (see U.S. government securities)
grace period, for loans, 160, 161
grandparent aid, 112, 115–117
grants, 101, 104–105, 107
guidance office, as source of scholarship information, 144–145

high school (ages 14 to 18), allocating investments for, 34
home equity loans, 160, 173–174
home mortgage refinancing, 174
Hope Scholarship Credit, 108–111, 146

improving aid eligibility, 132–136
income-contingent repayment plan, 166
income-sensitive repayment plan, 166
income vs. financial aid, 128

independent students and, 113
index mutual funds, 16, 25
inflation risk, 31
in-school payment of loans, 160
in-state vs. out-of-state schools, 112
institution-sponsored prepaid tuition plans, 60, 106–107
insurance policies, borrowing against, 172, 174–175
interest benefits of loans, 160
interest deduction, student loans, 167
interest rate risk, 31
interest rates, 19–25, 160
international mutual funds, 25, 35
Internet resources, 93
investment managers, prepaid tuition programs and, 62
IRAs, 21, 42–43, 176–177

junk bond mutual funds, 35

Kiddie Tax, 37

Leveraging Education Assistance Partnership (LEAP), 106, 135
life insurance as investment, 21
Lifetime Learning Credits, 108–111
line of credit, home equity type, 174
load mutual funds, 26
loans, 4, 6, 10, 101, 105, 107, 129, 159–178
local vs. long-distance colleges, 111
long-term investing, 16–18, 35
low income families, 139
lump-sum vs. monthly investments, 11–12

market risk, 31
matching grants, prepaid tuition programs and, 63
maturity, bond, 18–19, 20, 21
maximum account balance, in prepaid tuition programs, 62
merit scholarships, 141
merit-based financial aid, 124, 141
middle school (ages 10 to 13), allocating investments for, 33
military and military academies, 113
minority scholarships, 147
money market mutual funds, 25, 35
monthly vs. lump-sum investments in, 11–12

mortgage refinancing, 174
multiple children in college, 129, 139
municipal bonds, 20, 35
mutual funds, 19–20, 25–27, 35

need-blind schools, 138
needs-based financial aid, 124
negotiating better package, 138–140
Nellie Mae loans, 171–172

obtaining FAFSA forms, 131
ownership, child's name vs. your name for
    investments, 36–42

Parent Loans for Undergraduate Students
    (PLUS) loans, 6, 163–168
part-time college attendance, 111–112
part-time work, 114
pay as you go plans, 9–10
Pell Grants, 104–105
penalties, in prepaid tuition programs,
    51–52
Perkins loans, 159, 161
personal expenses, 5
personal financial specialists (PFS), 95–96
personal loans, 178
PLATO loans, 172
Plus loans, 126
portfolio management (see allocating
    investments and portfolio management)
premium price, bond, 19
prepaid tuition programs, state-by-state,
    51–60
pre-school (ages 0 to 4), allocating
    investments for, 32–33
principal, bond, 20
private loans, 168–172
professional help (see financial planners)
professional organization-sponsored
    scholarships, 146
Profile form, FAFSA and, 125–127, 130
public vs. private college, costs of, 4

qualifying for financial aid, 123–124, 129
ranks or tiers of colleges vs. cost, 2–13
references, for financial planners, 99
refinancing home mortgage, 174
religious groups scholarships, 146
Renewal FAFSA forms, 131

repayment schedules, federal loans,
    165–166
researching real costs, 7–8
Reserve Officer Training Corps (ROTC),
    113
retirement plans, 134, 172, 176–177
risk, 29–30, 35, 98–99
room and board, 4

S&P, bond ratings, 20
Sallie Mae loans, 105, 170–171
savings accounts (see also savings plans
    and 529 plans), 9, 107, 129, 134
savings bonds, 23–25, 35
savings plans and 529 plans, state-by-state,
    45, 46–61, 60–92
savings requirements, 8–13, 15
scholarships, 3, 4, 101, 105, 107, 141–157
    amount awarded, 142
    applying for, 150–152
    athletic scholarships, 147–149
    essay requirements and, 150–151
    Expected Family Contribution (FEC)
        and, 143
    financial aid gap and, 143
    need and merit combined, 142
    prepaid tuition programs and, 51
    rejections, top ten reasons for, 151
    requirements for, 142
    sampling of, 152–157
    savings from, actual vs. expected,
        142–143
    searching for, resources, 143–145
sector mutual funds, 25
SEP-IRAs, borrowing against, 176–177
services for scholarship searches, 145
short-term investing, 18, 35
Signature Education Loan Program, Sallie
    Mae, 170–171
Social Security, 135
Society of Financial Service Professionals,
    98
sources of funds for college, 107
Stafford loan, 159, 162–163
standard repayment plan, 165
state agencies for financial aid, 117–121
state aid programs, 106, 135, 146, 168
state ranking of college costs, 2, 52
stocks, 16–18, 27, 177–178

Student Aid Information Center, 132
Student Aid Report (SAR), 131–132, 131
Student Educational Loan Fund (SELF), 168
student loan interest deduction and, 167
student loans (see loans)
subsidized loans, 159, 162–163

Tax Benefits for Higher Education, IRS publication 970, 111
taxes, 129
   breaks in taxes for college savings, 107
   child's name vs. your name for investments, 36–42
   deciding on investment ownership and, 41–42
   deductions vs. credits in, 107–111
   Economic Growth and Tax Relief and Reconciliation Act of 2001 in, 109
   Education Savings Accounts (ESAs) and, 42–43
   Hope Scholarship Credit and, 108–111
   Kiddie Tax and investment ownership, 37
   Lifetime Learning Credits and, 108–111
   prepaid tuition programs and, 63
   student loan interest deduction and, 167
   Uniform Gifts to Minors Act (UGMA), 38
   Uniform Transfers to Minors Act (UTMA), 38
tax-exempt bonds, 20
tax-free tuition savings plans, 45
T-bills, 24, 27, 35
T-bonds, 24, 27, 35
TERI Continuing Education Loan (CEL), 169
The Education Resource Institute (TERI) loans, 105, 168–179
TIAA-CREF, prepaid tuition programs and, 62
time and compounding interest, 10–13, 15
timing, in investing/saving, 32
tips for completing FAFSA, 133
T-notes, 24, 27
tolerance for risk, 30

transportation, 5
Treasury bills, bonds, notes, 20, 27
trusts, Educational Needs Trust, 117
tuition and fees, 4
tuition savings plans (see savings plans and 529 plans)
two- vs. four-year colleges, cost of, 2, 111

U.S. government securities, 23–25, 27, 35
U.S. savings bonds, 35
U.S. Treasury Bills, 24
understanding financial aid forms, 128–130
unemployment, 139
Uniform Gifts to Minors Act (UGMA), 38, 115–117
Uniform Transfers to Minors Act (UTMA), 38
United Negro College Fund (UNCF), 155
University of Alaska College Savings Plan, 64
University Support Service loan program, 172
unlimited gift exclusion, 116
unsubsidized loans, 105, 159, 162–163

volunteer programs, 114

when to apply for financial aid, 130–132
William D. Ford Federal Direct Loan program, 162–163
work study programs, 4, 101, 105–106, 112–113
worth of college education, 5–6

zero-coupon Treasury bonds, 25, 35